RISK/REWARD

RANDOM HOUSE

NEW YORK

RISK / REWARD

*Why Intelligent Leaps
and Daring Choices Are
the Best Career Moves
You Can Make*

ANNE KREAMER

Published in the United States by Random House,
an imprint and division of Penguin Random House LLC, New York.

RANDOM HOUSE and the HOUSE colophon are registered
trademarks of Penguin Random House LLC.

LIBRARY OF CONGRESS CATALOGING-IN-PUBLICATION DATA
Kreamer, Anne.
Risk/reward : why intelligent leaps and daring choices are the best
career moves you can make / Anne Kreamer.
pages cm
Includes bibliographical references.
ISBN 978-1-4000-6798-5 (hardback) — ISBN 978-0-8129-9771-2 (ebook)
1. Career development. 2. Risk management. 3. Success in business.
4. Career changes. I. Title.
HF5381.K715 2015
650.1—dc23
2014046074

Printed in the United States of America on acid-free paper

www.atrandom.com

9 8 7 6 5 4 3 2 1

FIRST EDITION

Book design by Mary A. Wirth

For Mark and Heather

The central problem of our age is how to act decisively in the absence of certainty.

—BERTRAND RUSSELL

Improvisation involves coming into a situation without rigid expectations or preconceptions. We must keep going forward, fearful or not, and be ready for anything that comes our way. That's how life is.

—BOBBY MCFERRIN

CONTENTS

......................................▶

THE ART OF RISK

This is a book about risk. Not the adrenaline-spiking, bungee-jumping, double-or-nothing, high-stakes-poker kind of risk, but rather the risks that all of us with jobs and careers and professional ambitions do or don't take—and which we may or may not even be aware of as we proceed through our working lives. In the deeply uncertain and volatile American workscape of the twenty-first century, individual success and contentment depend upon developing and refining a regular habit of assessing *and taking* small and sometimes large risks.

Risk is most often understood as a negative, something foolhardy and always to be avoided. That's because we humans are evolutionarily conditioned to assume the worst when facing the unknown. *Is that berry poisonous? Is that a lion in the distance?* For our ancient ancestors, survival depended on the ability to infer a threat and make a split-second decision between fight and flight.

At the same time we're also wired to be cautious, to default to the familiar, holding our turf when facing dangers that are less acute. Our protohuman ancestors in east Africa lived in trees. But at a certain point, drought started destroying and shrinking their forests. No doubt for centuries they contemplated leaving their comfortable arboreal existence for life on the ground . . . and for centuries rejected that option because the dangers—think: lions—were more immediately terrifying than the slow-motion destruction of their age-old habitat. But having gauged the various risk factors over generations, our ancestors ultimately decided to come down out of the trees, accept the risk of predators and the unknown, and colonize the land—and, as it turned out, become human.

Today we mostly don't have to deal with the kinds of existential dangers that our ancestors on the African savanna or even in early America faced. But the current upending of the economic and social status quo and of the ways we've become accustomed to earning our living is definitely a threat.

When I graduated from college and started working fulltime in the 1970s, most of us expected we'd pick a career and stick with it for life, and working for decades for a single organization was still a common and reasonable scenario. Whether one was a lawyer, manufacturing line worker, teacher, salesperson, or reporter, there was an assumption of a clear, predictable professional trajectory. People anticipated they'd pay their dues, rise through the ranks, and retire with a fixed pension. There were risks, of course, but the risks tended to be short-term and specific—more lion in the grass than longterm drought.

That's no longer true. The working world has become a place where risk runs rampant: Secure jobs are becoming obsolete, the industries in which we've worked are disappearing altogether, entirely new kinds of businesses are arising overnight, pensions and other retirement benefits are disappearing, we are under constant pressure to stay technologically current, demands on our time in and outside the workplace are expanding—suddenly *all* these concerns are universal, chronic, and stressful. Even if you're someone who can reasonably expect to work in one discipline over the course of a lifetime, the need to respond and adapt to technological and organizational upheavals means your work is transforming at a rate similar to that of those who career-hop.

Circumstances beyond our control can quickly alter our jobs and expectations and long-range plans, for the worse or for the better and sometimes both—a company being sold, a start-up failing, a call from a headhunter, a pension reduced, a chance encounter on a plane with a potential investor, a pink slip. Keeping one's head down and doing the work competently used to insulate the vast majority of workers from job disruption, but today this approach is among the greatest risks of all. Today's working world is constantly fluctuating and fast paced. Jobs and job categories are being destroyed and created in a matter of a few years rather than decades, leaving behind people who are uncomfortable with change.

More and more of us, voluntarily and involuntarily, are making high-risk professional zigs and zags, jumping into the unknown of new working landscapes without much in the way of predictable outcomes or safety nets. The making-it-up-as-they-go-along, self-employed-in-multiple-freelance-jobs, who-knows-what's-next fraction of the population is growing fast. According to a recent MIT report, approximately half the jobs being created as the economy recovers from the Great Recession will be freelance; and according to a study from the financial services software company Intuit, 40 percent of us, maybe sixty million Americans, will be in some measure self-employed by the end of this decade. These are huge numbers. By the day, we are creating new businesses or professions that barely existed a decade ago. There's even a new term of art, "solopreneurs," that encompasses individuals designing apps, creating virtual stores, managing social media, and coaching people in their lives and work.

Multiple studies suggest that a young person starting work in 2015 must anticipate staying in any single job for an average of just four years and working at as many as a dozen different places over the course of an ever-lengthening working lifetime. And even those of us further along the professional track must assume that we may well be working at something quite different a decade from now.

The American economy is a reconfigured and reconfiguring one, and modern workplace threats don't have simple solutions. Job security for almost anyone at any level is a quaint twentieth-century artifact. Today, for most people, to do only one kind of work, let alone work for a single company, is often to consign oneself to disappointment or failure. Each of us is living in a new realm of ambiguity—which can result in an anxiety-producing chronic state of indecision.

In our working lives, when self-identity and financial well-being hang in the balance, most of us are conservative, reluctant to play the odds aggressively. Risk-taking at work used to be territory reserved for entrepreneurs, a slightly eccentric minority with a special temperament, bold or flaky or both.

Thirty-eight years ago when I started my career, I didn't think of myself as a risk taker. But I realize now, having repeatedly quit one job for the next and hopped from one industry to another, I was doing something different from that of most of my contemporaries, or at least those I knew. This was not a strategic decision. I had a wide variety of interests but no particular skill sets, and I felt no urgent calling. Rather than committing myself at the outset to one career, I experimented. My half-dozen distinct professional tracks (banking, international television, magazine publishing, consumer product development and marketing, independent TV production, journalism) and a dozen different jobs within those careers (assistant, sales, marketing director, business development, publisher, entrepreneur, producer, consultant, executive coach, public speaker, magazine writer, author) were all driven by opportunity (being in the right place at the right time to join exciting ventures—*Sesame Street, Spy* magazine, Nickelodeon); by trial and error and a willingness to start at the bottom again and again; and by a basic faith that, good outcome or bad, I'd cope.

Part of the reason I repeatedly made what I now see were risky professional decisions—what kind of person leaves a good job with nothing else lined up or even targeted?—is simply who I am. I've always been a fundamentally optimistic person, quick to make decisions and trusting in my gut to guide me in the correct direction. As one of two children from a middle-class Kansas City family, I also was brought up with a deeply ingrained sense of Midwestern can-do-ness—raised to believe that if I put my mind to something, I could figure out how to tackle the problem. My spontaneous temperament coupled with the if-I-build-it-they-will-come problem-solving mind-set gave me the confidence to quit job after job, often with nothing else on the horizon. At different times, different triggers were the catalyst: boredom, a sense of a lack of opportunity, feeling undervalued for endless hours of hard work or time on the road, a punishing workload, enthusiasm to be part of something new and exciting—or a combination of more than one of these.

I used to enviously watch friends graduate from law school and eventually become partners in their firms, or others become physicians after years of dedicated training, or my husband go from being an entry-level writer to an editor in chief in a decade. *How gratifying it must be to know what you wanted to do with your life! What was the matter with me that I couldn't stick with anything longer than a few years?* But now, more than three decades into my working life, I watch many of those same friends yearning to quit the inhumane 24/7 grind of practicing law in a big-city firm. Or doctors selling their practices because the U.S. health care system no longer seems focused on patient care. And others being laid off after decades of loyal work. As I see how the world has changed for those who once pursued the secure and steady career path, I no longer feel abashed by my zigzags, I feel lucky.

I always felt alien to friends who knew exactly what they wanted to be. I'm still wondering.

—DICK CAVETT

What once was viewed with skepticism—going wide and doing a variety of things versus going deep into one profession—can absolutely be a competitive advantage today. Particularly when we're young. A 2014 study by the National Bureau of Economic Research discovered that the younger workers who sampled more occupations—viewing each successive job hop as a chance to discover the kind of work they find most satisfying—tend to be more financially successful in their thirties and forties. Henry Siu, a professor at the Vancouver School of Economics, University of British Columbia, and one of the authors of the study, reported, "Job-hopping is actually correlated with higher incomes, because people have found better matches—their true calling."

I believe that amassing a range of skill sets and professional networks is a *requirement* to prosper in twenty-first-century work. This doesn't mean you can't or shouldn't aspire to work your entire life in one field, but it does mean that if you choose to be a lawyer, teacher, banker, architect, salesperson, or *whatever*, it is critical to keep abreast of possible changes in your profession. This notion of diversification can seem risky and counterintuitive in a world of increasing specialization, but specializing as a litigator, for instance, is not incompatible with maintaining an awareness of how those skills might be translated into different kinds of work: public advocacy and policy, educational reform, or work as an in-house counsel.

Over the years I've continued to develop new skills, forge new professional relationships, and allow new mental pathways that have served me well as each industry in which I've worked has been transformed. My multiple jobs in multiple industries have given me the chance to develop a variety of income streams; I like to think of it as having multiple legs on my career stool. I used to move sequentially from one position and industry to another—from television sales to textbook publishing to magazine marketing to toy development. Today I do multiple things *concurrently:* I write books, contribute to print publications, consult with various companies—and am developing a plan to launch a Web-based home-furnishings business with a graphic designer and partnering with another friend to develop a new media app. Each project is at a different stage of development, but the key for me is that if any *one* or even two of them were to disappear or come to naught, I'd still have other solid revenue streams.

> *He has half the deed done, who has made a beginning.*
>
> **—HORACE, *EPISTLES***

I know firsthand that today more than ever, the difference between professional success and failure lies in one's mastery of the art—and yes, it's an art—of taking risks. Today we *all* need to think and behave more like entrepreneurs. This is not your parents' working world. But even as the need increases for each of us to think more and more creatively and proactively and continuously about how to craft a satisfying working life, I think we have also become less and less certain about how to do that—or even of what kinds of possibilities exist. Ten years ago, if you'd asked mortgage brokers at Countrywide Financial or book buyers at Borders if they'd be in the same job in 2015, the majority probably would have said yes. And who could have anticipated a decade ago that they might be working for a massively successful company that enabled people to publish and share videos (YouTube) or digital snapshots (Instagram) or one that sells people a personal genetic analysis (23andMe)? "Our age of anxiety is, in great part, the result of trying to do today's jobs with yesterday's tools," Marshall McLuhan wrote—*in 1967,* when we still pretty much knew what tomorrow's jobs would be and our economy and culture had barely begun their accelerating process of thoroughgoing transformation.

THE RISK/REWARD STUDY

To get a deeper, and more than just anecdotal, sense of this shifting landscape and an overall insight into what Americans are thinking and feeling about work, I partnered with the research team at J. Walter Thompson, one of the largest advertising agencies in the world. At the turn of this century, JWT began tracking the things that were making Americans anxious. One of their consistent findings has been that at any given moment in time, about half of all Americans are feeling anxious about work.

In March 2012, January 2013, and May 2014, JWT and I conducted three national surveys of employed Americans, a representative sample (respectively 857, 800, and 650 respondents) of men and women in all fifty states working in a wide range of jobs and fields. We posed open-ended questions about the centrality of work to people's identities and the degree of control they felt they had over their working lives. The results were startling on multiple fronts. Only four in ten people think they will be in the same job five years from now. More than half are considering changing not merely their jobs, but their *careers*. Think of that: A *majority* of Americans are dissatisfied enough with their working lives that they seriously dream of an entirely new occupational path.

But there is a huge gap between the daydream of a new occupation and moving toward it, between *thinking* one needs to make a significant professional shift and actually *doing* anything about it. In our surveys, 46 percent of the people who want to change their jobs have not taken any concrete steps toward preparing for the lane changes they're contemplating. In the face of today's deep economic uncertainty, this is a dangerous disconnect.

We are restless. *And* we are paralyzed. So what's stopping us from moving forward?

We conducted these surveys as the economy was still only fitfully beginning to recover from the Great Recession, so it was no surprise that more than half of the people said that financial concerns inhibited their willingness to risk a job change. But the story is a lot more complicated than worry about paying the rent and car and grocery bills. Beyond the prospective financial risks of changing careers, these people described being held back because they don't have the time and mental bandwidth to explore new jobs or occupations. And among the younger cohort, "self-doubt" most commonly prevented respondents from pursuing new work, while a plurality of those in their fifties cited "fear of starting over" as the main obstacle to changing jobs or careers.

A whopping 80 percent of our respondents from all age groups said they were uncomfortable when faced with work-related ambiguity. This is troubling in an economy whose defining characteristic is uncertainty. And an increasing number of people in the prime of their working lives said they felt exhausted by the work-life choices they were obliged to parse.

In other words, we are not pursuing our dream jobs in large part because we're afraid, confused, and exhausted. And living in a perpetually fraught and anxious state, knowing fundamental change is coming but not exactly when or how, leaves many of us feeling anxious and drained as well as uninspired in our current jobs.

In my last book, *It's Always Personal,* I explored the subtle ways in which the neurobiology of emotion affects us at work. Similar to the findings of my new research with JWT, almost half of those we surveyed for that book reported experiencing fear and anxiety—key emotions involved in both avoiding and taking risks on the job. It is important to understand what this means in today's perplexing workscape. When we are exposed to something out of the ordinary, something we perceive as "risky," our bodies produce the stress hormone cortisol, priming us to fight or flee. This happens whether the new situation is actually threatening or merely unfamiliar. We wouldn't have survived as a species were we not hardwired to respond to potential danger. And that's okay when serious threats are few and far between—a kid dashing into the street to retrieve a ball or an annual performance evaluation—because our bodies can gear up, deal with it, and return to normal. But when we are constantly bombarded by the new, when the threats are ambiguous and chronic—as in so many of today's work environments—our bodies remain on high alert and in a state of constant negative arousal. This isn't a good thing.

Our ideal state for calculating risks at work is a sort of Goldilocks mode—too little change and we get bored, too much instability or upheaval and we shut down. When problems feel manageable and when we have the time and tools to process and understand our various options—when they feel like *challenges*—that's when we are operating at our best. A certain amount of uncertainty is good, keeping us alert, pushing us to think about change; but too much is overwhelming. To keep growing and remain employable, it's important for each of us to be aware of this delicate balance, a balance that requires both continually pushing boundaries of knowledge and competence and taking time for contemplation. "Jumping to conclusions," writes Nobel Prize–winning behavioral economist Daniel Kahneman in *Thinking, Fast and Slow,* "is risky when the situation is unfamiliar, the stakes are high, and there is no time to collect more information."

Where are the stakes higher and the information more ambiguous than in the choice of how to earn a living? And how *does* one figure out when to play it safe and when to take a leap? By experimentation. By embracing risk. Incorporating regular, modest gestures of risk-taking into our daily working lives is the first step toward navigating and thriving in this new landscape and working toward that dream job.

RISK AS A PRACTICE

The kind of risk-taking I'm talking about is thoughtful and continuous. It doesn't mean quitting a job on a whim, signing a lease on office space before drafting a business plan, or launching a product without a comprehensive competitive analysis. At the start it's modest and incremental, a matter of developing a continual *habit of mind,* a perpetual sense of nimbleness—which bit by bit and day by day will lead to significant change and long-term professional resilience and relevance. It means learning to ask questions of bosses and colleagues and peers day in and day out, developing an attitude of perpetual curiosity. It means getting out of your comfort zone to build vibrant networks of contacts. It means regularly crafting experiments to test new occupational notions. It means not just sucking it up and accepting the feeling of being undervalued in your workplace. It means sticking your neck out to try something new and accepting the possibility that you might fail. And after inevitable setbacks or mistakes, it means getting back up and at it, willing to try again.

It means visualizing your working life as if you're an acrobat, acquiring the assorted skills that make walking the professional tightrope a familiar thing, so that you are poised to leap from one trapeze bar to another, learning to accept the midair untethering between one gig and the next, praying your timing is good enough to make the catch, knowing how to fall safely if this time it is not.

In today's working world, our instinctual *fight or flight* responses still make sense—although in a much subtler, more complex, generally nonviolent, and not necessarily physical way. In this context, "fighting" doesn't mean hurting or scaring or yelling at other people. Rather, it means a willingness to see and confront and fix problems around you and in your own head, sometimes painfully—to fight to create work that *works* for *you*. And "fleeing" means getting out of your workplace, your organization, your field, to meet new people and discover new ways of working and thinking, because staying put is often a path to obsolescence—and, if necessary, it means *literally* fleeing, quitting your no-hope job or unsatisfying career.

Conscious, consistent, modest risk-taking will help you become more open, more able to recognize opportunity when it crosses your path, and more likely to seize the chance to make the right big change at the right moment. Regular risk exercises and experiments will help you find that sweet spot between having too little information to take prudent action and demanding so much information that you fail to take action at the opportune moment. By placing multiple bets of different kinds and sizes—meeting new people, learning new skills, freelancing or volunteering in new workplaces, having occupational sidelines—you will expand your network and understanding of your plausible options, minimizing the potential for any one misstep to be disastrous.

> *What's risky is realizing you've never terrified yourself with a flying leap.*
>
> **—ANNA QUINDLEN**

A regular practice of risk-taking *before* reaching now-or-never crises and inflection points of "I quit!" crises will help you develop a career *philosophy* and let go of the notion that you must have a perfect, fixed career *plan*. Such an inflexible life itinerary is increasingly impossible in today's working world, and instead I propose developing a mind-set of everyday self-reflection and an empirical practice of intelligence gathering and trial-and-error experimentation. Plans can and will be undone by factors beyond our control. A consistent philosophy of risk-taking, however, prepares us for the course corrections that we'll inevitably have to make to thrive in our careers.

To help get a better handle on what different kinds of risk look like, I traveled the country; I had conversations with people working in very different environments and at very different levels. I talked to highly successful people for their perspectives on the role risk-taking played in their careers. I probed the findings of academic and clinical experts for insight into behavioral economics and the psychology of choice. And I mined the extensive data J. Walter Thompson and I unearthed in an effort to understand the changing nature of work and risk today.

Risk/Reward is the synthesis of this journey. It's meant to be your guide to bridging the gap between just thinking and actually doing, with specific alerts calling out particular self-defeating behaviors and offering risk practices that will help overcome the inertia, the fear, and the confusion that prevent people from moving forward in work—and finding work that provides not just a paycheck, but pleasure and fulfillment.

RISK/REWARD

A CONVERSATION ON RISK:

Anna Quindlen

The Pulitzer Prize–winning writer Anna Quindlen, author of six novels and eight nonfiction books, took the big risk of leaving her prestigious *New York Times* columnist job at age forty-two. While "almost everyone seemed to believe it was to spend more time with my family," Quindlen straightforwardly credits the lure of becoming a "full-time novelist" as her catalyst. I asked her what she thought about risk in the workplace today, twenty years later.

What's the most significant risk you've taken professionally?

ANNA QUINDLEN: Here's what I consider risky professionally: Hanging on to a position because of fear or inertia and waking up one day and realizing you've missed forever the chance to try your change-up pitch. What's risky is realizing you've never terrified yourself with a flying leap. When you're feeling completely comfortable in a position, that's the time to move on. There are a hundred reasons not to do that, but they are all grounded in fear and convention. I think taking a job that scares the hell out of you is the key to success. It's how you grow. We're all like sharks: Keep moving or die. *Not a dead shark:* That's my mantra.

Chapter 1

THE RISK/REWARD MATRIX AND YOU

The data from my Risk/Reward survey research presented an eye-opening picture of how eager so many Americans are to transform their working lives and at the same time how stumped they are about how to enact the reinventions they imagine. What makes some people willing to leave good jobs and take those major risks? And what are the consequences of that behavior? Are some people naturally more comfortable with risk? How does nature fit in with nurture, temperament with training? What could I discover that would help people make better career decisions?

I understood how to think about risk from an evolutionary survival perspective—the kind that relates to existential threats: floods, earthquakes, and Ebola virus epidemics—with a layperson's grasp of basic statistical risk analysis. I was familiar with fairly straightforward financial risk assessment tools that help us decide if we are more comfortable investing in higher-risk/higher-return equities or lower-risk/lower-return vehicles such as stock index funds or bonds. But what about tools to help people facing *career* risks, such as whether or not to ask for a raise or promotion or different position at work? These decisions are impossible to quantify precisely and hard to make by means of simple rules, because they are so complex, involving components such as one's particular psychology, recent performance, age, tenure, rapport with the boss, and commitment to the organization and the culture and robustness of the specific organization and overall field. Did any sort of preexisting approach exist to help people decide how to calibrate these complicated workplace choices?

I thought personality assessment tools such as the Myers-Briggs Type Indicator could shed some light. Whether one is introverted or extroverted or analytic or intuitive certainly relates to one's baseline willingness to take risks at work. But as with IQ tests, I discovered that while basic intelligence and emotional range may partly shape one's appetite for and ability to deal with risk, their impact is only indirect and inferential. And a risk-taking predisposition does not follow a set path. There are plenty of people who behave riskily in one aspect of their lives but not in another—those who regularly drive over the speed limit, for instance, but invest their money in bonds or those who hop from one job to the next but have lived in the same modest rental apartment for decades.

This search for risk assessment paradigms and tools helped me get a sense of the complexity of risk. But I discovered no specific framework for measuring and examining it for individuals in the workplace. So I decided to create my own, which I call "the Risk/Reward Matrix." I again turned to the research team at JWT and also enlisted the help of Peanut Labs, an online market research firm, to help me craft a survey that would measure how we approach risk in our work and careers.

Risk is different for each of us and driven by different concerns at different stages in life. Some of us are born cautious; some of us are raised that way; some of us are naturally thrill-seeking lovers of adventure. Some come of age with every advantage, and others have to fight their way out of poverty or dysfunctional family situations. When we're young, changing jobs can feel easier. But at the same time, things such as shaky self-knowledge and student loan payments can hinder experimental decision making for younger people. In midcareer, we may think we know exactly what kind of work would be the most rewarding yet feel trapped by financial and familial obligations. And midcareer, too, a sense of paralysis can set in— so much has been invested in one path, jettisoning it can feel foolish and scary. Older workers often develop clearer insight into what is meaningful to them in work and have a good sense of where to find it, but they may feel limited by anxiety about having up-to-date skills or an adequate cushion for retirement.

To be alive at all involves some risk.
—HAROLD MACMILLAN, FORMER PRIME MINISTER OF THE UNITED KINGDOM

Based on my own work history and those of the people I interviewed, I believe we are motivated to take professional risks when we want more control or flexibility over how or where we do our jobs; when we want a new challenge; when we want to work with more interesting or exciting people; when we feel our values have been compromised or insufficiently linked to our work; when we want to earn more; or when we're simply bored.

I knew I had to plot the quantifiable aspects of work— salary, financial obligations, time spent at work versus leisure—against the more intangible. Does one's inherent appetite for risky behavior in everyday life translate into a willingness to flout rules and take risks at work? I also wanted to discover how people viewed worst-case work-related scenarios, such as getting fired—how likely they believed they were to experience these reversals and how well equipped they were to deal with the worst if it were to happen.

To explore overall risk tolerance—to find out whether people have a more or less fixed and fundamental "set point" for taking risks—we asked respondents a range of questions, including how often they did things like gamble, drive over the speed limit, attend events where they knew few people, or tell the truth even when they thought it might cause trouble. They could answer *often, sometimes, rarely,* or *never.*

Then we asked a series of questions specific to work and risk, asking respondents to what extent they agreed or disagreed with certain statements.

Here is a sampling from the survey. As you read the statements, imagine your own answers.

I believe success is more about luck and whom you know (being in the right place at the right time) than about hard work.

People say they'd like to run their own company; I'm the type of person who would actually do it.

If it were up to me, I'd work at many companies over my lifetime, not just 1 or 2 companies, but maybe 6 to 8 companies.

I always plan for the worst-case scenario.

I'm a person who likes to live on the edge.

The type of work that I do probably won't exist in 5 years.

I often think about switching careers and doing a different kind of job.

It is important that I feel valued at work.

I'd rather make less money and have more free time.

It would be very difficult for me to switch jobs.

I have no idea what kind of work I'm suited for.

To assess how prepared people felt to deal with career volatility, we asked how likely they thought they were to face a variety of setbacks over the next few years and how they might weather these setbacks. Here's a sampling:

Get fired from their job.

Not get the promotion hoped for.

Get promoted into a more stressful job.

Can't find work for a year.

Get a serious illness.

Have to work vastly longer hours.

Have to work for a demanding new boss.

Have to work two jobs.

Your company goes out of business.

You are transferred to another city.

We asked respondents open-endedly what their dream job was—and how difficult it would be to get that job and how long they thought it would take. And if they'd imagined starting their own business or professional practice, what did they imagine might be the biggest challenges in doing so—finding the right employees, raising money, running the office, being taken seriously in the field, dealing with uncertainty or stress, inconsistent cash flow?

> *In a time of drastic change, it is the learners who inherit the future.*
>
> **—ERIC HOFFER, AMERICAN PHILOSOPHER, RECIPIENT OF THE PRESIDENTIAL MEDAL OF FREEDOM**

We also wanted to find out whether people thought they had taken successful risks in their work and how often—and if they *hadn't* taken risks, what had stopped them. We asked what would motivate them to quit their current jobs, and for those who had changed jobs recently, we looked at what had motivated them to do so.

What emerged from the data were four distinct clusters of

people with shared attitudes and traits—in other words, four Risk/Reward personality types. I call them Pioneer, Thinker, Defender, and Drifter. You may instantly recognize yourself in one of these descriptions. Or you may find that you are on the cusp between two of them. Or that you've shifted from one type to another at different stages of your life. But they provide a framework, drawn from a representative sample of working Americans, for us to begin thinking about work and risk with fresh eyes. If you'd like to see where you fall in the Risk/Reward Matrix, you can take an abridged version of the survey at www.annekreamer.com/survey/risk before reading on.

> **PIONEERS:** 10 percent of people. Pioneers tend to approach work from the vantage point of "You only live once." They tend to be very decisive, and as far as work and career are concerned, they put a lot of chips on the table and are the most entrepreneurial of the four groups.
>
> **THINKERS:** 40 percent of people. Thinkers are the reliable, hardworking backbone of the workforce. They are theoretically comfortable with sensible risks but don't take many because of worry about finances and family stability. Many dream of going solo with their own businesses or professional practices but are unsure of the steps required. While often entrenched in their career paths, they nevertheless dream of changing jobs to find a greater sense of meaning and purpose.
>
> **DEFENDERS:** 36 percent of people. Those who fall into this group often occupy mid- and lower-level administrative positions. They like things to be predictable and tend to view their work as a

means to an end rather than a "calling." Most Defenders report that if they won the lottery, they would quit their jobs in a heartbeat. They resist change, preferring things to stay as they are.

DRIFTERS: 14 percent of people. Our research revealed that those who fall into this category tend to earn less, on average, than the other groups. But when we delved further into the data and expanded the research into one-on-one interviews, two distinct categories of Drifter emerged: *intentional* and *unintentional*. While there are ranges of attitudes and behavior within each of the four types, the differences between the two Drifter subtypes warrant calling them out more clearly.

INTENTIONAL: Intentional Drifters, those who consciously choose a free-form, freewheeling, improvisational approach to managing their career, are the smaller subset of this already small segment of the population. Intentional Drifters more often work part-time and self-identify as "craftsmen."

UNINTENTIONAL: Unintentional Drifters have ended up in less-than-satisfying jobs as a result of external forces. After decades of a shrinking manufacturing sector and declining trade union power and the Great Recession, these frequently blue-collar workers feel cast adrift, finding hourly jobs in the fast-food and transportation industries. Unintentional Drifters feel insecure, powerless, and abandoned by the American dream of upward mobility. They no longer feel that hard work contributes to successful outcomes and attribute any success they may have achieved to luck.

I've interviewed many people of each type (as well as the hybrids, such as Thinker-y Pioneers like me), and I will present some of their candid personal stories of work, career, and life throughout the book. I'll also discuss the scholarly research that bears on the four basic types. Each type—Pioneer, Thinker, Defender, Drifter—is predisposed to both certain pitfalls and inherent strengths when it comes to work-related risk-taking. I'll discuss how people of each type can exploit the opportunities implied by the particular strengths and how to compensate for the respective weaknesses by cultivating "risk practices" and developing a new Risk/Reward mind-set. While I've broken out the risk practices to address specific issues most relevant to each Risk/Reward type, everyone can benefit from adopting most of the practices.

Risk can involve feelings of danger, uncertainty, and anxiety as we grapple with the unknown. The Risk/Reward Matrix offers a framework for understanding your default response to uncertainty, and understanding and mastering this response is an essential step in learning how to proactively manage your career. In her autobiography, *Bossypants,* Tina Fey summed up her risk philosophy: "You can't be that kid standing at the top of the waterslide, overthinking it. You have to go down the chute." *Risk/Reward* will help you to find the right slide—and then to go down the chute.

A CONVERSATION ON RISK:

Po Bronson

Po Bronson is the author (with Ashley Merryman) of *Top Dog: The Science of Winning and Losing*. Their previous book, *NurtureShock: New Thinking About Children*, was on the *New York Times* Best Sellers list for more than six months. Bronson has also published five previous books, including *What Should I Do with My Life?*, a #1 *New York Times* bestseller.

What's the most significant risk you've taken professionally?

PO BRONSON: By the summer of 1999, I had been covering Silicon Valley for four years and had reached a certain prominence. My second book about it was on the bestseller lists, my face was front and center on the cover of *Wired* magazine, I had a big feature in *The [New York] Times Magazine,* and I was getting weekly paid speaking gigs. Despite all that, I had a nagging fear that if I wrote anything more about Silicon Valley, I'd become permanently attached to it. Joan Didion didn't keep writing about hippies after she'd penned *Slouching Towards Bethlehem* for *The Saturday Evening Post* in 1967. I didn't see the [bursting of the] bubble coming, but I persuaded myself that the cultural impact of the dot.com boom had peaked, and Silicon Valley would no longer be a cultural story, that it was becoming only a business story. So, despite 101 offers of assignment, I turned them all down and decided to do . . . *nothing.*

That was the hardest part of it. I didn't have my next idea yet. I didn't have another life raft to jump into. I did not harbor some other dream. I honestly had no hunch what was next. And it wasn't like I could afford to sit around—my wife and I had just tapped our entire savings to buy a house. But I had to create room for the next idea to germinate. For about a year, I wondered what to do with my life before I recognized everyone was wondering what to do with their life, and *that* was my next idea—I would do a book about that question.

Chapter 2

PIONEERS

In 2010, after a better-than-average fifteen-year professional run, at forty Brian Smith was feeling grim.

He'd graduated in the go-go early nineties from New York University's interactive telecommunications program and landed a job that he liked from the outset—producing and directing *Seeing Ear Theater* audio dramas for the Sci-Fi Channel's online site. As a kid, Brian had grown up listening to records of classic radio programs—*The Shadow* and *Fibber McGee and Molly*—and the opportunity to enter the suddenly *happening* cable industry *and* digital media, while also doing something inspired by the historical antecedents he revered, was perfect.

He established his professional bona fides and then, in 2000, channeling Anna Quindlen's "not a dead shark" keep-moving mantra, he left Sci-Fi to lend his expertise to another media sector. He took his audio production skills to book publishing, an industry *forced* to innovate, landing a job as the in-house producer of audio for Random House. He oversaw the audio production of Barack Obama's *Dreams from My Father,* working one-on-one with the prepresidential Obama in the studio—for Brian, a high point of his career. All the while, not content with just his day job, he had tinkered with writing screenplays—another of his childhood enthusiasms—and he succeeded in selling one that got made, *Alien Express,* starring Lou Diamond Phillips.

But in 2006, a few weeks before the birth of his first child, as the publishing industry responded to heightened competition, Brian was downsized out of his job. By most standards he'd been successful—working at prestigious companies in new media while also wisely maintaining a credible screen-writing career on the side. He felt confident that he could strike out on his own as a freelance audiobook producer while still continuing to write screenplays. Brian and his wife, Jackie Cuscuna, a full-time Brooklyn public school teacher, felt as though they were on their way to realizing their dream of what their ideal working lives might resemble. But then came the Great Recession.

"The audiobook business changed," Brian says, "and was brought in-house, and all of the freelance work dried up." He also found that "after writing the first few monster movies, the thrill of the work had diminished." Brian and his wife had been fortunate to sell their New York apartment before the market crashed, but he was increasingly anxious about living off their dwindling nest egg. Rather than drawing the rainy-day fund down to zero, Smith decided he'd go for broke and use the remaining capital to fund his own start-up.

Brian told me that he'd been kind of a weird kid and young

adult in the 1980s, "having a passion for old movies and radio plays and ice cream," and that he'd been "obsessed with wanting to live in the thirties and forties and run a soda fountain by day and work with Orson Welles and make radio plays together at night." While the dream of working with Welles was clearly a fantasy, Brian had actually produced radio dramas, and he believed that his dream of running a cool neighborhood ice cream parlor was something else he could bring to life. Brian "had no experience running a business" beyond his own freelance creative services work and "absolutely no background in the food industry." Instead, he had only his belief in his "vision to create a place in Prospect Heights, the [Brooklyn] neighborhood where people could gather with their families and eat the best ice cream in the world." Brian found his mission in his ice cream shop, which he named Ample Hills from a line in (Brooklynite) Walt Whitman's poem "Crossing Brooklyn Ferry": "I too lived—Brooklyn, of ample hills, was mine."

In partnership with his wife, he opened the shop in 2011. And promptly, lines formed around the block, winter as well as summer, day and night. And Brian thinks sometimes, Why? Why me? "This is always the great mystery, isn't it," he says, "trying to identify precisely why one place is more popular than another. Believe me, I have often sat and watched the line of people and wondered, What have we done, and can we do it again if we open somewhere else?" When pressed, he thinks there are two main reasons for the success of Ample Hills. One is the quality and playfulness of the ice cream. "The unique fun and funky flavors like Stout and Pretzels that you can't find anywhere else, and the quality of the ice cream, which comes from our dedication to doing everything ourselves, from scratch. We have a real passion for making ice cream, and I think people can tell that." The other thing he did that was unique—his competitive differentiator? "When we started, we were the only shop in New York City that made its ice cream on the premises, and in full view of the public, so as people waited in line they could see their ice cream being made." He thinks that people really appreciate this authenticity and transparency. "It's about more than just a place to get ice cream, it's a place where we invite you into the narrative of how the ice cream gets made."

WHY PIONEER?

In naming his business, Brian has deliberately invoked an era of growth and romantic invention for Brooklyn, and I believe he subconsciously associated his business with core attributes of the American DNA—the deep-seated belief in natural-born equality, political and economic liberty, and individual effort. During Whitman's life in the nineteenth century, the very word *pioneer* was new, and Americans were pioneering fresh geographic, industrial, and philosophical territories, opening boundaries for all kinds of people to find the fresh paths and new roles that suited them and thrive. Americans—raised with the conviction that economic advancement was attainable for anyone by means of hard work and ingenuity—plowed fields, laid railroads, mined gold, invented transformative machines, devised new schemes for manufacturing products and new schemes for selling them, built highways and glittering cities in seemingly no time from scratch. This can-do, think-differently mentality, deeply embedded in our national character, characterizes the most professionally nimble among us, even—or maybe especially—at this moment when the American dream can seem harder than ever to achieve.

Brian applied that can-do-ness in the way he rigorously studied ice cream to turn himself from a total amateur into a professional. "I went around to every ice cream shop in the city," he says, "and the tristate areas, taking notes, eating ice cream, watching customers, studying menus, seeing what others did well, what they didn't do well." And through his journey he was always "looking for organic, authentic ways we could be different, ways we could make our mark. If you don't do that due diligence, if you don't study the marketplace, and try to see where you can fit in, then you're inviting failure."

WHO IS A PIONEER?

They Change Jobs

Pioneers change jobs a lot—*significantly* more often than the other types: a whopping 38 percent in our surveys say that they have often switched jobs, compared with a mere 2 percent each of Thinkers and Drifters and 3 percent of Defenders.

Pioneers often embody the Silicon Valley mantra "Fail fast, fail early, and fail often." After all, the key take-away from

Darwinian evolution isn't actually that the strongest or even the (obviously) "fittest" survive, but rather the *most adaptable*. And given the incredible flux and uncertainty of the economy and work today, that's never been more true. When asked if they thought the organization they were working for today would exist in ten years, a large majority of Pioneers said no—while members of the three other groups overwhelmingly said the opposite. Nine out of ten Pioneers thought they personally would be doing something different five years from now, compared with only 20 percent in the other groups. Even if Pioneers are being overaggressive in their expectations of continuing flux and transformation, erring in that direction is by far the wiser course in this day and age.

They Are Diverse

You might assume that Pioneers would be the most highly educated group—people with a sense of confidence or entitlement who can afford to take more risks simply because of built-in safety nets, knowing they've got resources to draw on if things don't work out. But no. Among the Pioneers is the largest percentage of people who had graduated *only* from high school. Pioneers are also more ethnically diverse. Nine percent are African American, 20 percent Asian, and 19 percent Hispanic—compared with 5 percent nonwhite in each of the other groups.

It's not surprising to find that Pioneers are more likely to have started their own businesses—but more surprising, perhaps, is that they're also more likely to be senior executives.

They tend to live in urban areas and to congregate in parts of the country most amenable to innovation—47 percent of Pioneers live where the original, literal American pioneers headed, in the West and Southwest.

They Make More Money

While income is not the sole determinant in how successful people view their careers, it is the clearest benchmark. Pioneers' income on *average* is substantially higher than that of any of the other groups—mainly because more of them have exceptionally high incomes that skew their average upward. The average Pioneer has a household income over $77,000— 13 percent more than the average Thinker, 17 percent more than the average Defender, and 37 percent more than the average Drifter.

HOW TO BE A PIONEER

Put Chips on the Table

To use a gambling metaphor that Pioneers would like, they put more chips on the table and try their hands at different games. They move around and head down new occupational paths much more frequently than others. They use all aspects of their intelligence to arrive at a decision—their logic and their guts—and when they do decide on a particular course, they take action. They are not afraid to try something outside of their certified areas of expertise.

> *I have said and mean with all my heart I've only learned 1 thing "for sure" in 48 years: WTTMSW. Whoever Tries the Most Stuff Wins.*
>
> **—TOM PETERS, AUTHOR, *IN SEARCH OF EXCELLENCE***

Take Action

The ability to *act* is a significant differentiator separating Pioneers from the others. That willingness is a defining trait. When asked whether they agreed with the statement "People say they'd like to run their own company; I'm the type of person who would actually do it," nearly *every* Pioneer agreed, 98 percent. Pioneers do think critically about their work situations, but more than any other group they *do* something about it.

Pioneer Strengths:
- Anticipate change.
- Try lots of new things.
- Take action.
- Use logic *and* intuition in decision making.
- Work hard *and* turn off totally.
- Are flexible.

Think

While the gap between writing movies and opening an ice cream parlor might seem unbridgeable to most, Brian Smith didn't think so. "Believe it or not," he writes in his book

Ample Hills, "creating a movie monster isn't so different from creating a great flavor of ice cream. Really. If you're interested in monsters, you watch every monster movie you can get your hands on (preferably while eating pints of ice cream). You research mythical creatures—the Hydra, the Gryphon, the Cyclops. . . . You look up drawings of prehistoric beasts . . . You borrow the head of one, the tail of another. . . . You play around with it until it belongs to you and hopefully feels somewhat fresh and new.

"If you're interested in ice cream, you eat any and all ice cream you can get your hands on (preferably while watching old sci-fi and monster movies). You read ice cream cookbooks, cookie cookbooks, cake cookbooks. You walk up and down the aisles of the grocery store, studying ingredients. You borrow peanut butter from this flavor, honey-bacon cornbread from that one. You experiment."

> *Make something your own that matters to you.*
> **—BRIAN SMITH**

In this, Brian has produced the foundation of a perfect Pioneer manifesto. Study and explore everything you possibly can about what you're interested in. Experiment with the idea in ways large and small. Learn from mistakes. Try new things. "Make something your own that matters to you."

Fresh ideas tend to arise through trial and error and problem solving on the fly, while also thinking strategically, contemplating well-trodden pathways until that moment in the shower or on a walk when all the *thinking* synthesizes into something exciting and we say *Aha!* "Discovery," wrote Albert Szent-Györgyi, the Nobel Prize winner who discovered vitamin C (and fought in the Hungarian anti-Nazi Resistance during World War II), "consists of looking at the same thing as everyone else and thinking something different." This kind of iterative process—one that Pioneers practice instinctively—doesn't need to lead to some game-changing, world-historical breakthrough like finding a cure for heart disease or inventing a way to distribute music digitally. It can be deployed in the pursuit of something as simple and humble seeming as concocting the perfect salted crunch caramel ice cream. As Brian puts it, "You experiment. You play around with it until it belongs to you, and hopefully tastes somewhat fresh and new."

Experiment

Brian didn't invest their life savings until he felt he'd perfected his ability to make exceptional ice cream. Jackie, his wife, "pushed the idea that we have a food cart and sell the ice cream in smaller bits." She was actually less concerned, he says, "with whether the ice cream being tested was perfect than in finding out if her husband wanted to make ice cream every day." They started conservatively, in 2010, with a food cart. And that "act small but think big" phase convinced them both a) that they could make ice cream that people loved, *and* b) that Brian reveled in the new work that was seemingly nothing like the producing and writing he'd spent his first twenty adult years doing.

The food cart beta version of the business, he believes, also meant that he got more truthful feedback before opening his store, without "the veneer of a fancy shop." It was easier for a friend to tell him that the cookie in the ice cream didn't taste very good when they were eating in his kitchen, when the new business was still a highly provisional, DIY work in progress. And by doing this, he learned to *listen* to the criticism. "I do think it's a critical part of success for entrepreneurs, to have the ability to listen. You have to be willing to jettison the stuff that [isn't part of] your core values—like making a sausage-and-caramel ice cream. You have to be willing to listen to your audience."

Feel

All the hard work and preparation is useless unless you have an ironed-out sense of meaning or purpose when it comes to decision making. The true test of Brian's Pioneer spirit came on the eve of opening his first Ample Hills storefront.

One week before signing the lease on their first store in 2010, he "got a call from a book publisher asking me to run their audiobook division for a higher salary than I'd ever been paid before, with benefits, holidays built in, and the security of working for a big company." If the offer had come six months earlier, it would have felt like precisely what he should do—an irresistible gift from the universe. But after months of investigation into how to launch his business and developing the confidence to take such a major step, and six days from "the point of no return," the job offer threw him into a tail-spin. He spent twenty-four excruciating hours "with the devil on one shoulder, and an angel on the other," wrestling with the decision. To do or not to do?

A rational person, he thought, would obviously choose the secure option, the corporate job. He was convinced that Jackie would want him to accept the offer. With two kids to support, it was the grown-up thing to do, right? It was absurd to indulge a dream when they had a sudden "escape hatch" so perfectly suited to his experience and proven skills. Some friends told him to go for it: " 'You can always come back to Ample Hills after you've socked away some dough.' I don't know if this is an early-twenty-first-century thing, but I believed that I have a right to happiness, and that I have a right to pursue that above the security that our grandparents and parents [sought]. Ultimately I had the sense that I had to go for it and that you only live once. The weaker decision would have been to take the publishing job."

Beyond YOLO, a few things tipped him in favor of the ice cream store dream. No doubt the most essential was Jackie's unwavering faith in him and their shared vision. "If we open the shop," she told him, "maybe we'll struggle, maybe we'll just squeak by, maybe the kids won't have as much stuff—but they'll have a happy dad." She said she didn't want to live with Brian always asking himself, "What if, what if?" The choice was also made easier because after thinking about the offer, Brian realized that even though he would be paid an amazing salary, he was being asked "to come in to lower the costs of producing audiobooks and decrease the quality—it was kind of a hack job in the end" that he knew wouldn't be fulfilling.

And with so much change and consolidation happ~
publishing industry, how could he be certain that the ,
that seemed so secure today wouldn't be eliminated in a couple of years? He knew that making ice cream "made me
happy." Plus, Jackie had her relatively secure job as a school-
teacher.

Today, four years after signing the first lease, Ample Hills
has sixty-five employees and has opened a second venue in another up-and-coming Brooklyn neighborhood. Brian's energized by his work and is eager "to find a way to expand and
keep the core creative and community values that we've in-
stilled so far." I asked whether he thought he'd still be selling
ice cream ten years from now. "It's hard for me to see myself
doing the same thing the rest of my life, but what I enjoy about
this ice cream stuff is that it's different every day, there is a lot
of stuff—designing new shops, creating new flavors, managing the people—that keeps it exciting and different."

Balance Analysis with Intuition

Brian's approach to decision making—developing a devotion
to acquiring the skills and knowledge needed to perform one's
chosen work at the highest level and connecting that knowledge base to feeling—is *the* key way in which Pioneers are different.

Crucially, Pioneers don't rely on a single way of viewing the
world and making decisions. Pioneers make decisions based
on a balance between serving their emotions and the reality
check of logic and fact. Each of the other groups relies much

more on logic in figuring out the right moves to make at work. This is a critical distinction.

> *The artist is nothing without the gift, but the gift is nothing without the work.*
>
> —ÉMILE ZOLA

Psychologist Gerd Gigerenzer, director of the Center for Adaptive Behavior and Cognition at the Max Planck Institute for Human Development in Berlin and an expert on risk, says that "a gut feeling is neither caprice nor a sixth sense, nor is it clairvoyance or God's voice. It is a form of unconscious intelligence"—in other words, a judgment based on underlying reasons that one has perhaps not yet fully articulated to oneself. A Pioneer's ability to tap into these important but semiconscious or unconscious understandings is what gives him or her a critical edge, the confidence to know when and how to take action.

But how is a prudent, rational person to do that? Brian tapped into his childhood dream of "going back in time to be a soda jerk at an ice cream parlor."

Two decades ago, with the publication of his book *Descartes' Error: Emotion, Reason, and the Human Brain,* Antonio Damasio, the head of the University of Southern California's Brain and Creativity Institute, upended our long-held notions about rational behavior. He and his wife, Hanna, a professor of psychology and neurology, conducted research persuasively showing that *emotion* is as essential as pure rationality in making sensible decisions. With the introduction of the functional magnetic resonance imaging (fMRI) machine, scientists have been able to observe the living brain in real time as it makes decisions and have verified the Damasios' insight that without the tempering commonsense effect of inarticulate emotion (*Do I* feel *more like wearing a skirt or pants to work? Would I rather make ice cream and hang out with people in my neighborhood or write screenplays in a room by myself?*), it is impossible to make the simplest decisions. People who have damaged orbitofrontal cortexes—a part of the brain integral to regulating emotion—lose the ability to make choices.

Pioneers have the ability to come into new situations with open-mindedness, without rigid expectations or preconceptions, using their intuition to guide themselves through professional zigs and zags by moving forward *improvisationally.*

Why does the ability to shift back and forth between analysis and intuition matter so much to our working lives? Because today, in this highly fluid economic and social and technological moment, things rarely lend themselves strictly to a linear, logical, purely quantifiable plan. For most of the past two centuries, by-the-book rationalism was the basis upon which businesses and careers were built—if we do A, then B will reliably follow. And today, where big data are wishfully regarded as game-changing and actionable X-rays into the habits of consumers, logic-driven analysis is being granted even more salience in organizations' decision trees. But this approach gets you only so far. Data and logic are important to making or rejecting risky choices, but one's information is inherently incomplete, and overreliance on the analytic often provides only a comforting *illusion* of control and predictability. It's but one piece of the complicated equation driving successful ventures and successful working lives.

Which means that we cannot rely on logic or numbers alone to chart our careers. By ignoring your gut, searching for answers *only* in the data, you may never feel confident enough to act. By the same token, with *only* a passionate dream you may not be able to act because you fret—correctly—that you haven't done enough analysis. When you combine both, as Pioneers do more naturally than the other three Risk/Reward types, when a choice is correct it really, really *feels* correct. As Brian Smith told me, the choice to open Ample Hills was "from one perspective a huge risk, but to me it felt like the only thing that we needed to and should do." It came to seem the most obvious "way to create something that adds value to the world, something that can make a mark. Pretty clearly I wasn't finding that in my screenplays."

Purely rational people might not choose to be a war correspondent or an infectious disease expert. When *The Wall Street Journal* asked Christiane Amanpour, international correspondent for CNN and ABC News, why she took the risks she did, she said, "Being a foreign correspondent can be a risky profession, but if my son decides that he wants to be a journalist, I would love that. Because this job comes with great risk, you have to have passion and commitment." Anne Rimoin, an associate professor of epidemiology at the UCLA

Fielding School of Public Health, is fueled by the possibility of stopping or containing the next pandemic, saying that to do so "is well worth the risk." Work for these kinds of extreme risk takers is not just a job, but a mission as well.

Furthermore, in his book *A Whole New Mind*, author Daniel Pink observes that the analytic "left brain" skills that were the great drivers of industrialization and the launch of the information age are no longer adequate. He argues that a new conceptual age is arising, one suited to explorers and experimenters—dare I say Pioneers? Paraphrasing Samuel Taylor Coleridge, Pink says that the successful mind must be androgynous, nimble, and multidexterous. He warns that many left-brain, linear, task-oriented occupations—accountants, lawyers—will sooner than later be automated, replaced by algorithms embedded in microchips, and that what will be essential for a human being crafting a good working life is the ability to put all the hard facts of a situation into *context*—to be able to *tell compelling stories*. Christiane Amanpour and Anne Rimoin have internalized this tenet. To be successful, we need to integrate our analytic side with our instinctive side more seamlessly—or, as Pink says, to put the text into context. In other words, to be more of a Pioneer.

Know the Value of Doing Nothing

Pioneers know how to exploit something else exceptional that *none* of the other groups do. And it's something completely at odds with our on-call-24/7 culture. Pioneers understand that they need to thoroughly refresh themselves if they hope to maintain their alertness and their willingness to keep forging new paths. Almost half of the Pioneers reported that sometimes they do *nothing at all.* What heresy! How dare they?

So simple a concept, yet so hard to achieve. Americans have been acculturated to believe that we're wasting time if we aren't *producing,* and as a result we take fewer vacation days than people in any other developed country. But Pioneers know and *act* on the knowledge that narrow input yields narrow output.

Executives who spend all of their waking hours hermetically sealed in the office environment—going from meeting to meeting or traveling by town car to airport to cookie-cutter hotels the world over—haven't a clue about their customers, who they really are, what they really need, what they really think of the product the executives' companies provide. Almost *all* Thinkers, Defenders, and Drifters say they are pretty much unable to disconnect, turn off. And they do this at their peril. Working or thinking about work all the time puts us at risk. We lose sight of the fact that new ideas are often triggered by the surprise and messiness of real life. The other three groups rarely move beyond the familiar, whereas almost four out of ten Pioneers say that they often go to new neighborhoods or travel to developing countries and regularly eat unfamiliar food.

Tony Schwartz, godfather of the "work in ninety-minute cycles for maximum productivity" movement, is an outspoken evangelist for taking full stops away from work. When he stumbled across the notion of "periodization," a practice elite athletes use to manage their work-rest ratios, his life changed. Periodization enhances performance in athletes, something even we non-elite athletes who regularly work out understand. Heavily taxed muscles and organs need time to recover to maintain or increase strength and stamina. The same idea is absolutely applicable to our working lives.

THE DARK SIDE OF RISK

But as with everything, too much of a good thing can be problematic. There's a downside to risk associated particularly with the Pioneering personality, when one too fully indulges the inner thrill seeker. Neurobiologists have discovered a particularly insidious kind of feedback loop that can plague and undermine risk takers. When we compete and take risks, our bodies produce testosterone, women's as well as men's (although men produce far more). Once we begin to experience the hormonal jolt of energy and focus that accompanies a risk, especially a successful one, we crave more and drive ourselves to take additional or greater risks—compelled by the primal biological need to keep feeling that jolt. In his book on risk-taking and the financial industry, *The Hour Between Dog and Wolf,* the Wall Street trader turned neuroscientist John Coates writes that "at low levels of testosterone an animal will lack motivation, arousal, energy, speed and so on, but as testosterone levels rise so too does the animal's performance in competitions and fights. When testosterone reaches its high point on the curve, the animal enjoys optimal performance. It is in the zone. However, should testosterone continue to rise, the animal begins to slide down the other side of the hill, and its risk-taking becomes increasingly foolish." Too much prolonged production of testosterone leads to "overconfidence and rash behavior."

Pioneer Weaknesses:
- Indulge in greater overall risky behavior—for instance, gambling, driving too fast, drinking too much.
- Excessive aggression.
- Too demanding.
- Hubris.

In trying to tease apart the forces that contributed to the financial meltdown of 2008, a team of researchers from the Departments of Physiology, Neuroscience, and Business at Cambridge University discovered that the higher the levels of testosterone in financial players, the greater their risk-taking. The study suggests that the heightened levels can "shift risk preferences and even affect a trader's ability to engage in rational choice."

Coates writes that testosterone in particular is present during our "moments of risk-taking, competition, and triumph, of exuberance." This may explain why, in our research, almost two-thirds of Pioneers are male. And it also suggests that neurobiological differences between the genders play a role in one's predisposition to take or avoid risk (see Sheryl Sandberg, *Lean In: Women, Work, and the Will to Lead*).

The kind of aggression associated with some kinds of risk-taking at work may also explain why Pioneers were by far the most fired of the four groups, 39 percent reporting that they had been let go from a job. Yet they tend to be clear-eyed about accepting responsibility: Two-thirds of the Pioneers who had been fired say it was *their fault*. Too much conviction, too much passion, too much appetite for risk, can overpower the balancing force of reason in one's decision making and cause a cascading emotional chain reaction that makes it very hard to put on the brakes. If it's a night of overindulgence in alcohol, the consequence might only be a killer hangover. But it might also be serious—an unhinged and cruel remark to a friend, risky sex, a DUI. The same is true of risk and work. Pioneers need to be vigilant, staying aware of this pedal-to-the-metal tendency to overdo.

NATURE VERSUS NURTURE: CAN YOU CHANGE YOUR TYPE?

As I'd started thinking about risk and work, I wondered if those who took more risks in their work were more intrinsically daredevilish in general. More often than the other types, according to our research and as I had hypothesized, Pioneers do engage in risky "lifestyle" behavior. These findings echo what Temple University psychologist Frank Farley has also uncovered: that there are clear personality traits that correlate with an appetite for risk. Farley labels those who seek more adventure and stimulation "Big T" types—more extroverted, creative, and risk oriented. On the other end of the spectrum are the "Little t" types, people who prefer routine and apparently safe situations. Most of us fall somewhere between the two poles, and a propensity for risk-taking is not necessarily fungible across the different areas of one's life. For all of my professional risk-taking, for instance, I *always* wear the seat belt in taxis and *always* get to the airport two hours before a flight. Ditto for Brian Smith. He honestly has no idea where his appetite for professional risk-taking comes from. "I don't jump out of airplanes, I've never snowboarded, I've led a fairly square life. It's not like I'm some *Wolf of Wall Street* kind of thrill seeker."

So I've pushed myself to become a bit more logical, analytic, and careful in taking on new professional pursuits. Thrilling new research in neuroscience is revealing how mutable or "plastic" our brains are in response to our environment. Indeed, while we are likely born and raised predisposed with a novelty-seeking "set point," I also believe—and this is one of the key messages in *Risk/Reward*—that we can *train* ourselves to think and act in more optimal risk/reward ways. And for most people, that means training to venture more enthusiastically, and successfully, into the uncharted territories that more and more of contemporary working life is becoming.

> *Change will lead to insight far more often than insight will lead to change.*
> —MILTON ERICKSON, AMERICAN PSYCHOLOGIST

NURTURE

This is where the nurture part comes in. When I interviewed people who'd changed jobs often, I asked whether they felt there had been something in their upbringing that had encouraged them to take chances. Most said yes, but there was no consistent pattern to the risk-taking that was encouraged—or modeled, negatively or positively. Each person had a different take. "I was raised to believe that life on Hester Street is still way better than in a shtetl or Communist China," one very successful son of Chinese immigrants told me, mixing his stereotypical Lower East Side ethnic metaphors. "There's a fundamental work ethic, an immigrant drive, as it were, in my family that hard work will allow me to live in a place better than the one we'd left." Some people watching parents ground down in unhappy jobs, unwilling to reach for something better, were motivated to be different—vowing that they would have the gumption to quit or strike out for the frontier, as it were. Other people talked about growing up in unstable families, where parents were divorced or ill, and how powerfully that had driven them to take care of themselves. One woman told me, "I had to create myself as a person, due to some very challenging parental issues. I started working in eighth grade and really viewed work as my best place for self-expression."

Conversely, growing up in solid two-parent households where one or both parents had a steady job can foster a sense of security that encouraged some of my interviewees to feel comfortable taking risks—they believed someone would always have their back.

Pioneer Risk Practice Tool Kit:
- Broaden focus outside of self.
  — Solve someone else's problem.
  — Volunteer for a cause that isn't directly tied to furthering one's career.
- Find mentors or co-workers from other risk styles who counterbalance natural Pioneer "Just do it" exuberance.

DISCOVERING YOUR INNER PIONEER

Ted and Gail Scovell are inspiring exemplars of the truth that even if one's professional arc seems clearly charted and predictable from an early age, our appetite for work-driven risk rarely follows a single trajectory but is fashioned in response to life stage and circumstance.

If we learn to listen to the nudges from and encourage our inner Pioneer, we have the potential to shift from one modus operandi into another, and *large course changes are possible*—several times over a lifetime.

Gail graduated from Harvard Law School and became a corporate tax lawyer in New York City, her hometown, following in her father's footsteps. She was good at her job, and regardless of how dull others might imagine corporate tax work, she found it "the most intellectually challenging thing I'd ever done." In her twenties, she thoroughly enjoyed her work, her colleagues, and her firm. But at thirty, six years into the typical eight-year track to make partner, and two years after marrying Ted, the pleasure was palpably diminishing, and she didn't want to "work around the clock," the way she saw the partners doing, even on weekends and holidays. She says she "talked about leaving and talked and talked, and didn't do anything about it until Ted said, 'You can leave or you can stay. But you have to stop complaining or else do something about it.' That triggered something in me."

Like Gail, Ted was feeling similar dissatisfactions. He'd stumbled into a Wall Street job—a kid sitting next to him in a class during his senior year in college had told him that Morgan Stanley was a good company and was on campus recruiting—and without much further thought he went into finance. He found he was good at it, but after four different jobs in the industry, eventually winding up at Bankers Trust as a proprietary trader, managing investments for the bank itself rather than clients, Ted was bored. And stressed. "There's something about buying and selling that's just not fulfilling [to me]," he says. With the twenty-four-hour trading cycle, he felt he could never entirely leave his job. He'd developed facial twitches. He was ready for a change. So . . . "If you want to quit," he told Gail, "you pick the time and I'll pick the place." At which point two quintessentially left-brain people—analytic, prudent, conventionally successful—started flexing more to their unrulier instincts.

In college a decade earlier, Ted had studied ants under the great biologist E. O. Wilson and had spent a couple of weeks in Costa Rica helping a graduate student from Wilson's lab who was researching Formicidae in the wild. He'd been captivated by the country and now, restless at thirty, recalled the sense of wonder and peace he'd had while living there. So Costa Rica became their rat-race escape hatch destination. Ted didn't just arbitrarily throw a dart at the map and end up in Whereverstan; he knew firsthand what they might expect from Costa Rica and felt that his earlier fascination with biology might lead to a professional reinvention. It was emotion, deliberately accessing the memory of how happy he'd been while living there at twenty, that cemented the decision.

Having lived well below their means in a modest apartment, Ted and Gail had enough savings to bankroll a radical experiment. In 1995 they both quit their prestigious, high-paying Manhattan positions and moved to Central America for a year. Ted and Gail had a plan—but a sensibly flexible, very loose plan. "We could have been there three months or the rest of our lives," Ted says, "but the deal was, whoever wants to come back first just had to say it and there'd be no argument. We had an open-ended frequent-flier ticket that we knew at the end of the year we could use for a move back [to New York] or a vacation. All we committed to was to house-sit for a friend [in Costa Rica] for three months." They managed their financial exposure and risk by subletting their New York apartment, using frequent-flier miles, and house-sitting to minimize the initial Costa Rican outlay.

Ted says his colleagues were not particularly surprised, although he says they did think he was "brave to quit the job to go hang in the cloud forest with no stress." On the other hand, when Gail announced the plan to one of her firm's partners, he told her, "That's the *stupidest* thing I've ever *heard*." Which demonstrates another quality of Pioneers: 91 percent of them say they know themselves well, and 90 percent say that if the worst were to happen in any given situation, they figure they could land on their feet. This gives them the confidence to strike out on a path contrary to conventional wisdom that their peers might find too terrifying even to consider.

Gail and Ted each describe the experience as "transformative." The tiny town in which they lived, Monteverde, was settled in the early 1950s by American Quakers who'd refused military conscription and after serving prison time for their beliefs had gone into exile as dairy farmers. Even in the 1990s, the town had extremely limited phone service and no paved roads. Quakers were still there, as were biologists studying and trying to preserve the cloud forest. It was "not utopia," Gail says, "but I hadn't met a group where so many people were thinking about why they were doing what they were doing, nor so many who lived in the moment. And this sounds incredibly trite, but I liked being with my husband and not being passing ships in the night." Ted still marvels at the salutary full stop in his life. "I had a garden, I went to Quaker meetings, I read one hundred books" in a year. "It literally changed the way I look at the world. In New York you keep your head down and look at the sidewalk. There you look up and are constantly surrounded by beauty. I was already a conservationist when I arrived, and I became a crazy one while living there."

Nurture Your Emotional Self, Embrace Variety

The Scovells' full stop mirrors the high value that Pioneers place on allowing themselves to nurture different aspects of their selves. Pioneers and the other groups all work hard in roughly the same proportion, but Pioneers are singular in their willingness and ability to *turn off* completely. Gail and Ted's time in Costa Rica shows the benefit Pioneers derive from their ability to stop work and restore themselves—rebooting, nurturing, or newly discovering aspects of their essential selves. It's a concept that positive-psychology researchers have found is central to increasing one's odds for contentment: *variety*. Pioneers embrace variety.

When we are habituated to the same things, we tend to become bored, disengaged from thinking about our futures and ourselves in fresh or intriguing ways. According to the research, experiencing the novel, using new skills, and overcoming unfamiliar challenges can punch our psychological reset buttons, permitting us to feel renewed enjoyment in life. It's something that psychologist Mihaly Csikszentmihalyi (the godfather of the idea of *flow*) has studied extensively. He's observed that "whenever we discover new challenges, whenever we use new skills, we feel a deep sense of enjoyment." Injecting variety into our lives can also create windows through which unimagined opportunity can find a way in.

I really enjoy the unknown and uncertainty. I like when things are up in the air or changing. That's where I tend to feel most comfortable.

—STEVEN MOLLENKOPF, CEO OF QUALCOMM

And that's exactly what happened for Ted just six weeks before the end of their stay, when he was asked to work as a substitute biology teacher at a local school. "I ended up loving it. And decided to become a biology teacher when we came back to New York." As Gail remembers the time in Costa Rica, "You sit there and say, 'Who *am* I? What do I care about? And how do I define myself if not by the superficial tags that I've used to define myself before?'"

Be Flexible

Ted and Gail are also excellent examples of how risk-taking doesn't require that we operate at adrenaline-inducing full throttle for the entirety of our lives. Pioneers are responsive to changing circumstances. Navigating life successfully demands that we listen to our inner voice and obey it when it tells us to pull back. Ted and Gail, for instance, agreed to end their experiment when they decided to have a child. "Ted might have been willing to have a kid in a town with no paved road or health clinic," Gail says, "but I was way too much of a city kid, and wanted to be in a place with top medical facilities."

After a year away, Ted and Gail returned much clearer about

who they were and what they wanted. "It was much more of a culture shock coming back to New York," Ted says, "than it had been going down to Costa Rica. It was really bizarre being in a city after being in place where we had wasps and ants and lizards and chameleons living in the walls, and no media to speak of." Ted followed the path he'd stumbled onto in Costa Rica, becoming a biology and math teacher—and at a Quaker school, Friends Seminary in Manhattan. Gail left tax law but did not choose to abandon the law altogether, instead becoming general counsel for the Guggenheim Museum.

It's a Lifelong Process

In 2005, as they turned forty, not quite a decade after returning to New York City from Costa Rica, Ted and Gail Scovell again felt the itch to shake up their lives. "If the twentieth-century career was a ladder that we climbed from one predictable rung to the next," author Jocelyn Glei writes in her book *Maximize Your Potential,* "the twenty-first-century career is more like a broad rock face that we are all free-climbing. There's no defined route, and we must use our own ingenuity, training, and strength to rise to the top." There are thousands of different jobs and ways to integrate those jobs with the life of a partner. By having radically and successfully shaken up their working lives once—activating their inner Pioneers—Ted and Gail were primed to do so again. And their second shake-up illustrates how different catalysts affect us differently at different stages of life.

The first time, boredom and a kind of "forever young" restlessness had been key drivers. This time, for Ted, the death of his mother brought back his carpe diem mentality, and he and Gail thought that living in a different culture would be a great experience for their son, then nine. With a finite stay planned this time and with more preplanning involved than on their first foray, Gail quit her museum-lawyer job, Ted arranged for a one-year sabbatical from his New York teaching position, and they returned to Costa Rica. Once again Ted was able to teach at the Monteverde Friends School, and this time Gail followed suit, becoming a substitute math teacher when another teacher suddenly quit. Gail says their experience with a child "was in some ways even better." Their son, more naturally sociable than they, "would charge ahead into any situation and we had no choice but to follow along. We made far more new friends through his openness." And, she says, "we saw different things there through a kid's eyes. As he learned about the army ants in our house, we did too."

Back in New York today, the Scovells know they've been very lucky. "When you go off and do this crazy thing," Ted says, "new opportunities open up that you'd never have anticipated." After his initial, successful eleven years in the financial industry, "the chance of ending up a teacher was so incredibly small—and it's the best job in the world for me. I love it." Although Gail says she is naturally more conservative in her outlook than Ted, she knows that their lives "are richer" as a result of their stints in Costa Rica. She has been surprised and grateful that neither of her absences from the major league working world were a problem during reentry job interviews in New York, neither back in the 1990s when she was in her thirties nor more recently in her mid-forties. Like most Pioneers, she trusted that she would land on her feet. And she found that if she responded to interviewers enthusiastically and *briefly* about her off-the-grid experiences, they just moved on.

Gail's experience with teaching in Costa Rica goaded her once again to tweak her career track. While still practicing law, on her return she shifted the focus to education, becoming general counsel at Hunter College, part of New York City's municipal university system. But recently she felt the urge to stretch further, becoming general counsel for the Open Society Foundations, a nongovernmental organization devoted to strengthening the rule of law and respect for human rights around the world.

Gail's and Ted's experiences demonstrate the benefits of adopting Risk/Reward habits large (moving to another country to explore new horizons) and smallish (transitioning from one type of law practice to a variety of others). And their willingness to shake things up again and again is reflective of today's mutable workscape, where at all stages of life it may be incumbent upon us to stretch leaving our comfort zones.

Be Willing to Be Lucky

No conversation about taking risks would be complete without a discussion of the role of luck. Pioneers are open to and appreciative of luck. According to our surveys, they believe that a large part of success can be attributed to knowing the right people and being in the right place at the right time. But can we increase our odds for good luck? In his great essay

Here Is New York, E. B. White memorably noted that ambition and success require "a willingness to be lucky," which is not a matter just of passively *wishing* to be lucky.

Loosely defined, luck is something that occurs accidentally or randomly (or, if you're of a mystical bent, by destiny or Providence) and benefits one professionally or personally. The longer the odds of the particular twist or turn happening, the greater the significance we'll assign to our sense of how "lucky" we've been.

> *Chance favors only the prepared mind.*
> **—LOUIS PASTEUR**

I think of luck much in the prepared mind way that Louis Pasteur did. It's obvious we can increase our chances of being disastrously unlucky by taking certain risks—by riding a motorcycle without a helmet or starting a business without doing any market analysis. What's less obvious is that we can *increase* our chances of being lucky by taking certain professional risks—Ted's luck in finding out how much he loved to teach, for instance. Or me leaving a well-paid job at CBS (which I'd gotten because of a lucky conversation with a friend) to help my husband start *Spy* magazine, then leaving *Spy* to join *Nickelodeon* (a job I also got because of a lucky conversation with a friend). In *Great by Choice,* Jim Collins writes that putting oneself in the way of lucky happenstance is a discipline. I couldn't agree more. It's the discipline of being out in the world—exploring new terrain, meeting new people, risking trial-and-error experiments, and falling on our faces—that increases the odds of *fortunate* twists and turns occurring. In other words, it's what Pioneers do—they plan, but they also *feel* their way into new jobs.

Jane Pauley

Jane Pauley was a cohost of the *Today* show from 1976 until 1989 and of *Dateline NBC* from 1992 to 2003, and in 2004 she hosted *The Jane Pauley Show*, a syndicated daytime program.

What's the most significant risk you've taken professionally?

JANE PAULEY: Put professional risk-taking in context. I never expected to have the career I had. *Today* show at *twenty-five*? There's a story there. Also when I left thirteen years later. And thirteen years after that—when I left *Dateline*. That event was more unambiguously voluntary, so *TV Guide* called me "the poster child for Second Acts" and Barbara Walters called to ask, as many did, "Why walk away from a prime-time show?"

My answer was that I simply felt there was more for me, but I wouldn't know what it was until the TV camera got out of the way and I said I understood that "more" would likely mean less. The irony was that all the attention I got about leaving made me more valuable to NBC—so I was quietly offered a daytime show. This was definitely more, not less. And there was the TV camera again!

But it was a different kind of TV than I'd ever done. A live audience.

Women, mostly. A conversation. I was intrigued. But scared, too. I'd always worked with a partner, if not an ensemble. This would be just me.

I was dithering over this decision even while *Dateline* was preparing a special "Jane Pauley Signs Off" [segment]. Michael J. Fox was my final *Dateline* interview. I asked him a long question about how even with Parkinson's he still did so much—a new book, a TV pilot, a fourth child, and raising $17 million for Parkinson's research—in just the last year!

"If it was me," I said, "I'd be relaxing, conserving my energy."

His response: "And what would you be conserving your energy *for*?"

It resonated so powerfully. And I think that was the precise moment I decided to say yes [to the new daytime show].

Going up against Oprah I warned my kids that this was a long shot, but that I defined success as having the courage to try.

Remember [when] Oprah gave everyone in her studio audience a new car? That was the week my show debuted. Within weeks it was obvious it was not going to be a success under any but the above-stated terms.

The show was canceled after one season. It was the hardest year of my professional life. And the best. I'm proud of the shows we did. One critique [was that] it was "too much like NPR." But we had fun, too.

I have a poster from *The Jane Pauley Show* prominently displayed in my home office. My psyche seems not to know it was a failure. That younger woman in the picture inspires me, because she had the courage to say "yes."

Chapter 3

THINKERS

As the daughter of a butcher from the Bronx and the grand-
daughter of Latvian immigrants, Mindy Shapiro, among the
top pulmonary specialists in the country, did not start life as-
suming she'd be a doctor. But her family, like the majority of
Thinkers, placed enormous importance on education, compelling her to excel. After graduating from the selective Bronx
High School of Science in New York City, she went to Harvard
College, then the Johns Hopkins School of Medicine, and finally did a fellowship at Yale University. As the oldest of three
daughters and "being the son my father always wanted,"
Mindy zeroed in early in her life on a goal that she thought
would make her family proud—becoming a doctor. Like the
Thinker she is, Mindy worked diligently and single-mindedly
to achieve her professional goal.

After a decade of higher education, she reached a "forma-
tive decision" not to go into academic medicine. Instead she
began a rigorous analysis to determine the best place for her
to establish a private practice treating people with lung disor-

ders, her chosen specialty. Las Vegas, not a city that would come to mind first, given her background, was a perfect bull's-eye for what Mindy wanted. On paper it was ideal—"they breathed different air." In the late 1980s, the city was a bonanza of opportunity for a young doctor—expanding at a rapid rate, with a dry climate that attracted a large population of retirees and people with pulmonary illnesses such as chronic obstructive pulmonary disease.

Despite her thorough research into the optimal place to practice her particular kind of medicine—logic-based decision making being central to Thinker behavior—Mindy says that when she arrived in Vegas, her reality was very different from what she'd imagined. "I felt like I was in the second reel of *Gone with the Wind,* like Atlanta after Sherman's March—everywhere I turned there was construction, and I felt like I was a carpetbagger and deep out of my culture, on the farthest planet from where I'd grown up." Was it a huge risk for a driven, self-made, Ivy League–educated single eastern girl? For sure. "But it was also a very calculated risk. It seemed perhaps excessive to my parents, but I knew that the portability of my profession—that all the tools required to do my job well are in my head—meant that I could always backtrack to more familiar turf." It wasn't the Pioneer's blithe faith that *something* would come along, but the Thinker's carefully hedged Plan B.

WHO IS A THINKER?

Focus

A large majority of Thinkers believe that they have one overriding skill or passion that defines who they are professionally, and that laserlike focus from the start is essential. A Thinker's clear and paramount sense of a *goal,* a particular brass ring and a careful plan to grab it, removes much of the doubt that can slow forward momentum in building a career. Daniel Goleman, the pioneer of the idea of emotional intelligence, recently published *Focus: The Hidden Driver of Excellence,* in which he quotes Yoda from *Star Wars:* "Your focus is your reality." Focus helps people plan for the future—to decide to become a doctor, a magician, an accountant, or a professional athlete—and gives those in pursuit of a specific career a long-range perspective that helps them to keep going when faced with the difficulties required (training, practice, experience) in realizing their goals. This long horizon line explains why more Thinkers than any other group, one in seven, have advanced degrees. Even more than Pioneers, Thinkers derive meaning and satisfaction from their work. While Pioneers clearly believe in multitasking, Thinkers may have the ultimate career edge in their predilection for selective, longer-term attention. The ability to focus is a significant competitive advantage that Thinkers bring to work. Their knack for focus helps Thinkers, more than the other groups, find and concentrate on the signal and ignore the noise. If Pioneers tend to be sprinters or decathletes, Thinkers are the working world's marathoners.

> *Your focus is your reality.*
>
> —YODA

Hard Work and Reliability: Grit

Working hard and being reliable are the other two key defining traits in the Thinker's career tool kit. Thinkers keep at it tenaciously. Hard work and reliability translate into what's increasingly being recognized as a significant determinant in success, what's known as grit. Grit is an absolute prerequisite for maintaining career momentum in today's highly competitive and highly uncertain environment.

University of Pennsylvania psychologist Angela Duckworth has studied the drivers of success that fall outside of a quantifiable baseline level of intelligence. And by studying a range of people from West Point cadets and national spelling bee finalists to classroom teachers, she's been able to identify precisely how grit, or its lack, accounts for a significant variation in individual success. According to her research, "The achievement of difficult goals entails not only talent but also the sustained and focused application of talent over time." Duckworth's insight perfectly embodies an essential attribute of the Thinker mind-set and behavior. If you'd like to test your own grittiness, you can take an online test from the Duckworth Lab at https://sites.sas.upenn.edu/duckworth. The notion of grit is critical to any conversation about work and success, because our ability to focus these days is being challenged as never before. Even absent a clinical diagnosis, most of us feel as though we are suffering from some kind of attention deficit disorder.

> *Your living is determined not so much by what life brings to you as by the attitude you bring to life; not so much by what happens to you as by the way your mind looks at what happens.*
>
> **—KAHLIL GIBRAN**

Thinkers, therefore, are more suited to harnessing their willpower in the pursuit of their vocation. More than any other type, Thinkers self-describe as being consistent in their behavior, which allows them to master a skill, to develop a plan for what comes next, and thus to keep progressing within their chosen field. Thinkers are also the perfectionists of workers, with fully 80 percent of them saying they always do only their best. Their self-discipline and consistent hard work are rewarded. Organizations value and self-employment requires people who reliably show up and have the stick-to-itiveness to get the job done, day in and day out. Thinkers are the second most highly compensated group of people among the four Risk/Reward types.

But one of the most interesting and surprising single findings in our research was the discovery that although a quarter of Thinkers describe themselves as members of the professional and management class, the highest percentage of all the groups, in our sample there were *no* Thinker C-suite executives—zero. This is not to say that Thinkers cannot achieve the highest levels in organizations. Many do, several of whom I spoke with at length. But our sample starkly illustrates a strong tendency of which all Thinkers need to be aware and—if they aspire to run large organizations—develop countermeasures to overcome. By diligently doing their job, Thinkers sometimes fail to recognize and seize the chance to take on new, risky-looking challenges—they are too busy trying to take impeccable care of business as usual.

Thinker Strengths:
- Focused.
- Reliable.
- Consistent.
- Hardworking.
- Educated.

At thirty-three, Mindy Shapiro was rewarded for her other-directed standard of excellence when she landed a desirable job in her field, but it was her habit of hard work and reliability that served her when she found herself the youngest doctor in a well-established group practice where the three senior partners were married men in their fifties—all of whom, as it happened, drove Hondas. "My commonality was that I also drove a Honda."

Talk about a fish out of water. A young, single, female physician in Las Vegas. But like a true Thinker, she rolled up her sleeves, did her work, and focused on the outcomes. She adapted to the foreign environment, working hard for years to earn the formal right for a shot at becoming a full partner. But to her dismay, the conservative, Honda-driving older men's answer was no. "I'd been raised to express what I thought, and that was what had made me successful in the past. But in this situation that was just not a good thing."

Mindy says she learned something essential at that moment—that particular organizations prize particular personality attributes in addition to sheer knowledge and competency. "I learned the lesson that I have to keep on learning over and over again, and understand: that being smart isn't always predictive of success. Being nice, being socially correct, being what people expect, is often more predictive of success in a work group than just being smart."

Three years after making the considered but risky move to Las Vegas, she was forced to decide whether to try to find a position working for another established practice in Vegas, move back east, or stay in town and strike out on her own. Over the course of a long Fourth of July weekend, she sought the advice of her local friends and mentors and decided she was ready to hang out her shingle. She leapt—but she looked carefully and, in Thinker style, meticulously devised a plan. A few weeks later, she started working short-term with another group of doctors, and within the year she had opened her own practice.

CAN A THINKER BE ENTREPRENEURIAL?

Thinkers have *considered* working for themselves, starting their own businesses or professional practices, almost as much as Pioneers—61 percent of them, versus 64 percent of Pioneers. But pulling the trigger to take action is harder for Thinkers.

> *If opportunity doesn't knock, build a door.*
>
> **—MILTON BERLE**

Fifty-three-year-old Benjamin Dyett is a vibrant example of a highly educated Thinker who found the profession in which he worked, as "a mild-mannered lawyer who worked at a number of law firms where I specialized in real estate law," not particularly fulfilling. Benjamin had grown up in the 1960s, the son of "the first black doctor to be admitted to practice medicine in a hospital in Westchester," and as Benjamin describes his dad, "he was a small-business man and was *out* there." But it took a while for his dad's risk-embracing mindset to flower in Benjamin. In 1986, Benjamin graduated from New York University School of Law, having chosen a career that required significant focus and effort and that had clearly defined goalposts for advancement. He worked in law firms in real estate for seven years but in 1993 realized he found the traditional law firm structure constricting and went solo.

When he struck out on his own, like a prudent and careful Thinker, he took many of his real estate clients with him. But the one thing he couldn't quite figure out was how to work independently while also presenting himself in an environment comparable to the old-school burnished-wood hushed law firm offices that his tradition-bound clients associated with successful practitioners. When in-person meetings were required, he found himself asking friends to borrow office space or renting executive suites around New York City for a day or a week at a time. The options weren't great in the 1990s and early 2000s. "In many cases I found myself in a dreary windowless office with a conference room down the hall that had all of the charm of a grim breakout meeting room in a midlevel hotel." The rented spaces felt like loser-y backwaters, the kinds of places to which laid-off executives were exiled as part of their outplacement packages and the exact opposite of the dynamic go-getter image Benjamin wanted to project. It was in such a place that he had the epiphany that would change his life.

"I had a minor problem, maybe a light bulb was burnt out, I honestly don't remember, but I went to the manager of the space I was then renting and asked him to take care of it, and he looked at me with the attitude of 'We could care less about your problem.'" The space was fully occupied, the decor barely presentable, and Benjamin realized that "if these knuckleheads can make a business of this with terrible execution, with a little effort and new thought, I could do this better."

He was tired of solving every tiny logistic problem on his own, tired of feeling isolated from other people, and tired of working in a place where he felt embarrassed to bring clients. "I figured if I needed it, other people needed it, too." He leased nine thousand square feet in the Flatiron district of Manhattan and in 2011 launched Grind, a collaborative work space and co-working community in New York City. "Grind came out of necessity, but I realized I also had a larger mission. I wanted to facilitate a revolution in the way people work." For $40 a day or $550 a month, 60 to 120 Grind members—a community of entrepreneurs—work in a light-filled, elegantly designed, loftlike office where all of their needs are taken care of, from Wi-Fi to conference rooms to coffee and cleaning and maintenance to a business mailing address. Two more locations opened in 2013, one in Chicago and one in New York City's garment district, and more are scheduled in New York for 2015.

As Benjamin describes it, the people who come to Grind "don't want job security, they want career fluidity." In other words, many customers are Thinkers like Benjamin in his past life, seeking to turn into the Pioneer that he's become. Benjamin opened Grind in the right place at the right time—capitalizing on the burgeoning class of self-employed, telecommuting workers in technology, media, fashion, and consulting. These are people who "network endlessly and collaborate constantly," he says, what he calls "free radicals." I spent time at Grind and discovered a huge range of people: freelancers and entrepreneurs, creatives and lawyers, accountants and techies. As one member told me, "You get to interact whether you want to or not." Its vibe is exuberant and quasi-communal, the very opposite of loser-y.

Benjamin's experience in real estate law and his Thinker's habit of focus were ideal preparation for the business he ended up creating. Going in, he was fluent in the ins and outs of the main asset of his new business—real estate—able to find and negotiate deals for space as a pro. He enlisted a childhood friend to be his main partner, and they started "with a blank sheet, writing what we wanted the story of the company to be." Benjamin believes every successful project or brand has a distinct point of view and that the most successful ones stick to that vision. "Apple was started by a guy on a quest to change the world, Red Bull was a company that had a distinct point of view, Nike is a company that has a philosophy about fitness and living life that everyone wants a piece of. And then there's a company like Toms, whose whole purpose is bigger than shoes, it's about changing the world and helping people and getting involved in everything around you—that company is about so much more than shoe profits."

Grind's mission, as outlined in that road map four years ago? "Abolish friction. High-tech, low stress. Work how you want, when you want. Superior sustainability. We're in this together. Grind isn't ours, it's yours. Open space for open minds."

CAN EVERY THINKER BE ENTREPRENEURIAL?

But not all Thinkers who test-drive being entrepreneurs make the transition permanently. For the first few years after Mindy opened her own practice in Las Vegas, it seemed like her dream had come true. She felt she'd found her professional sweet spot, "like running a marathon and I'd finally hit that rhythm." She'd proved to herself "that I could start again and that it didn't feel like a terrible risk to me. The money started coming in and patients were happy and I had confidence that I'm doing it and this is how it's done." She says she felt a new inner security and that she once again "had a good game plan in place." Thinkers typically thrive when they have a clear direction and focus to ground them in their work.

But once the health care system began its dysfunctional unraveling in the nineties, she was unable to keep following her road map. She had made the decision to set up her old-fashioned "non-Walmart-like" practice at a time when there were enough patients who valued that kind of individual care for her to make a living. But soon she found she was swimming against the tide. As the health care business consolidated and became further industrialized, she found herself forced into making decisions for her business at the expense of her patients. "Part of it was this horrible dichotomy—am I ordering this test because the patient actually needs it, or am I doing it because the patient needs it but it would be financially helpful to me, too?" For instance, she says, "If you did a breathing test on the same day that you saw a patient, you didn't get paid for the breathing test, but if you did it the day *before* you saw the patient, you'd get paid for it. So I ended up asking my patients to come to the office twice, which was a huge inconvenience to them. I found myself thinking that I didn't want to spend the rest of my life dealing with those stupid kinds of rules." She says she "realized I just want to be a *doctor* and not have to worry about that kind of stuff." She wanted to get rid of the running-the-business part of her job and return to her *focus,* helping sick people, which was why she'd become a doctor in the first place and what she felt she was best at.

She approached this challenge in logical Thinker fashion—by sending her curriculum vitae to a wide range of managed care corporations. Today she works north of San Francisco in Santa Rosa for Kaiser Permanente, the pioneering nonprofit, and has minimum management responsibilities. She's one of fifteen thousand Kaiser Permanente physicians, but she is energized by her work, feels collaborative with the one hundred pulmonologists at the other twenty-three Kaiser Permanente facilities in Northern California, and has been able to narrow her focus once again to what she loves about her profession. She's found that with her "decades of medical training, all the information and experience settles, and there emerges a sort of clarity. There's all this static around you in the hospital, patients and their family telling you stuff, and you're listening, but somehow there's this space where you can filter it out and you just *see clearly.* There's this intense focus and things become really clear."

> *Where your talents and the needs of the world cross, there lies your vocation.*
>
> —ARISTOTLE

Successful Thinkers like Mindy use their central attribute, that propensity to *focus,* to navigate the ups and downs of their careers *and* the day-to-day here-and-now tasks of their jobs.

HOW THINKERS GET STUCK

Many Thinkers don't understand that their great strengths, their determined focus and relentless work ethic, can become their Achilles' heel. Too much focus can be risky.

Given how hard it is to advance professionally, I had assumed before our research that competition for entry into upper management roles would necessitate a dedicated, singular focus. But it seems that while focus is an essential quality up to a point, if one's objective is to run an organization, adopting a more flexible approach to getting there seems to be even more important. A tendency toward *narrow* focus, I think, is one of the reasons why 39 percent of Thinkers—more than in any other group—reported that they "haven't really gotten to where I hoped to be."

Thinker Weaknesses:
- Too focused, lose the forest for the trees.
- Burned out.
- Don't trust instincts.
- Blind to opportunity and unconventional left-field options.

The Trouble with Narrow Focus

According to behavioral economist Daniel Kahneman, intense concentration on one task or topic shrinks our perceptual field, essentially blinding us to what others would see as obvious. In *Thinking, Fast and Slow*, he cites as an example the famous experiments first conducted in 1998 by psychologists Christopher Chabris and Daniel Simons. In this experiment, people were asked to watch a video of a basketball game intently, counting the number of times the ball was passed by players in white while ignoring the players in the black jerseys. Midway through the videotaped scrimmage, someone in a gorilla costume walked across the court for nine seconds. Almost half the viewers concentrating on how many times the ball was passed *did not see* the person in the ape costume. You can see Chabris and Simons's selective attention test at http://www.theinvisiblegorilla.com/gorilla _experiment.html.

How does this matter in thinking about what we ought to do for a living and how we ought to do it? One way that the perceptual blindness that Chabris and Simons call "inattentional blindness" crops up in the workplace is an inability to envision alternative scenarios or solutions. If you've spent years doing one kind of work—selling cars, teaching science, administering mammograms, managing restaurants, whatever—you may have so narrowed your focus about the nature of work at which you can excel that nothing else seems plausible or available to you. Maybe after a decade in one line of work, like advertising sales, you've lost the capacity to imagine how the people-reading skills that got you into sales in the first place could translate into a job in human resources for a tech company. I'd spent two decades working in the business world when the editor of *Fast Company* asked me to write a column—which started me thinking of my knowledge and experiences and *potential* competencies in a very different way.

Narrow Focus and Burnout

By any measure, Margaret Roach has been diligently focused and successful in pursuit of her chosen career, journalism and magazine publishing. Margaret climbed the editorial ladder rung by rung—a classic Thinker pattern—establishing her journalism bona fides as a young sports copy editor at *The New York Times,* then jumping to editor in chief of the start-up magazine *Women's Sports,* then to New York's *Newsday* as its fashion and garden editor, and finally, in 1995, going to join "that woman with the glue gun," as her bewildered colleagues said at the time—that is, Martha Stewart, at her eponymous magazine. Margaret grew with the company, eventually becoming executive vice president/editorial director, overseeing the Martha Stewart Living Omnimedia magazine, books, and websites.

She was focused, reliable, and hardworking—the consummate company woman. Unmarried, she devoted every waking hour and no doubt many dream hours to helping build the company. But that blindness came at a personal cost. After fifteen years, she felt burned out.

She'd known for a while that she wasn't entirely happy in

her work, but again and again she'd pushed down her discontent, staying the course. More forward thinking and experimental during her first two decades working, in middle age she'd become incapable of seeking her career path in a fresh way.

Once we feel comfortable in a decent, well-paid job, it's extremely hard to make a leap into a new kind of work and generally harder at fifty than it is at thirty. The familiar, even a familiar that has become unsatisfying, is hard to relinquish. It is a truism in psychology that the pain of potential loss looms larger than the pleasure of potential gain. It became almost impossible for Margaret to envision anything different.

As for how she spent that decade and a half at Martha Stewart, and about roads not taken, Margaret confesses to a few queasy "what ifs" when probed today. She is by her own description a loner, whose idea of perfect bliss is mucking around by herself in her garden and who "loathes networking." But Margaret wishes she had chosen growth and discomfort more often—that she'd been more active in industry organizations and attended more events, that she'd met more people both for purposes of "networking" and as possible models for an alternative working life. As she says, keeping her nose to the grindstone "made me a great corporate first lieutenant—someone who worked for the brand's good—but I probably didn't further my own creative mission to the degree I could have." In hindsight, she thinks, her corporate years in particular prevented her from "appreciating my own writing ability."

> *To refuse the call means stagnation. What you don't experience positively you will experience negatively.*
>
> **—JOSEPH CAMPBELL, PROFESSOR OF COMPARATIVE RELIGION**

Eventually, at age fifty-three, Margaret summoned the courage to quit. And today, seven years after quitting her executive job, her regrets have receded. She's reinvigorated her original journalism focus, and she hasn't abandoned her fundamental Thinker self but has in addition embraced her inner Pioneer—the one that led her to leave solid corporate jobs at twenty-five and forty for uncertain start-ups—to start her own one-woman online company, A Way to Garden (as she calls it, "horticultural how-to and woo-woo"). She runs it from her home in rural upstate New York. And she's rebuilt those atrophied writing muscles, publishing two books about the price she paid working in corporate America and the redemption she found returning to her figurative and literal roots.

ESCAPING THE FOCUS TRAP

Elastic Focus

Thinkers I interviewed outside of our survey sample, people who *have* achieved senior operating roles in their organizations, have figured out ways to adapt their focus to changing circumstances, practicing something I call "elastic focus." People who continue to grow in their professions have learned to tap into what Daniel Goleman calls "open awareness," a specific kind of focus that he says is a form of attentiveness characterized by "utter receptivity to whatever floats into the mind." For Thinkers in particular, who always crave a *plan* for their work and career trajectories, the most apt metaphor might be what cinematographers call "rack focus"—as the camera moves during a shot, they adjust the lens focus from a face to a street outside the window behind it, or from a driver to the landscape she's passing through.

How and Why Elastic Focus Works

I was first exposed to what I now understand as elastic focus as a teenager, when I was taught to ride a horse with what my teacher called "soft eyes." Soft eyes means that as you ride you try to be *peripherally* aware of everything going on in your field of vision—widening your scope at the edges to loosely take in the full landscape—the fallen tree trunk that might harbor a rabbit that could dart out and startle your horse, the grove of wildflowers where stinging bees might lurk, the loose gravel on the trail. I was taught that it's only by softening one's perspective that one can take in the whole picture and antici-pate potential challenges that might arise. Soft eyes allow a rider to be relaxed yet simultaneously alert and present. Pre-cisely the right frame of mind for today's workplace—aware of the larger picture yet able to take care of the day-to-day.

If you want to get a sense of what elastic focus might feel like without riding a horse, try this experiment. Wherever you are right now, gaze intently at one object, such as your coffee cup. You'll notice that when you really focus on one thing, it's to the exclusion of everything else in the room. Now widen your vision, soften your gaze, allowing yourself to be at least a little conscious of everything else in the room. See the difference? Staring only at the coffee cup is tunnel vision.

Northwestern University psychologist Mark Jung-Beeman, who studies brain behavior under stress, has discovered that if someone is *too* focused and on edge, his or her ability to solve a problem is actually reduced. Let me repeat this: *Too much focus can produce a kind of paralysis.* Barbara Fredrickson, a psychologist at the University of North Carolina, has studied this phenomenon and found that negative emotional content, the kind that stresses us out at work, tends to produce a more constrained, narrowed focus—while positive feelings stimulate areas in the brain that broaden one's field of vision and sense of options. In other words, when we are stressed we imagine fewer alternatives.

> *It is the ability to choose that makes us human.*
> —MADELEINE L'ENGLE, AUTHOR OF *A WRINKLE IN TIME*

Open Awareness in Practice

John Eyler, Jr., the sixty-seven-year-old former CEO of FAO Schwarz and Toys "R" Us, described just such a moment when he told me about how a once-in-a-lifetime chance to test his mettle forced him out of his comfort zone. In 1983, a little more than a decade after being hired into the May Department Stores Company training program directly out of business school, he had methodically risen through the ranks to become CEO of one of May's divisions. He was approached by Federated Department Stores, the owner of Macy's and Bloomingdale's, to found an entirely new division that would directly compete with a California-based chain called Mervyn's. Mervyn's had carved a successful niche for itself by offering discounted "soft goods"—clothing, bedding, towels—in no-frills stores in shopping malls. John was comfortably running his division for the May Company, and the logical next step would have been to take on a larger division for May. "I had been with the company for twelve years and had a bright future with them. It made no sense to leave that to go to a competitor to start a business from scratch." Along with the majority of his fellow Thinkers, his first inclination was just to stay put.

But then he pulled his focus back, taking in a larger view and listening to his emotions. The opportunity to "develop something from scratch," he started to think, "to build my own team, to define it, to create the culture of the new company . . . tapped into the entrepreneurial spirit that had been simmering in me. It's one thing to get a division to perform, and something else entirely to *create* something for the then premier department store in America." John also knew that he would not be jumping without resources: He'd have direct access to Federated's CEO, the necessary capital, and a chief operating officer from inside Federated who knew the ropes—factors a Thinker would consider important when making a decision. "When I left the May Company at thirty-five, I was by far the youngest person in top management—the next youngest principal was fifty—so the opportunity to lead that company was very real. I realized that what it held for me was doing more of the same thing on a larger scale, but that it basically wasn't interesting enough for me to spend my life doing that." John closely fits the work-hard, nose-to-the-grindstone, rise-through-the-ranks Thinker profile, but when the right opportunity appeared he was able to think bigger—considering but then overcoming his naturally conservative inclination—and seize the chance. And his elastic focus no doubt contributed to his ability to rise to the highest levels of management.

Like other Thinkers who have taken the plunge, John says that the experience surpassed his expectations. "It was incredibly fun. We started with one employee and in eighteen months had opened the first of our eighty-thousand-square-feet stores with a full distribution center and organization. It was like putting on a pair of track shoes and running as fast as you can." The decade at Federated allowed him to build on his accumulated experience to oversee and design every aspect of the new venture, from the moldings used in the store interiors to the merchandising strategy to the organizational structure.

The decision to leave a company in which he'd grown up, with all the attendant risk, was a turning point in John's life. After Federated sold his division, he went on to revitalize the FAO Schwarz brand and was able to facilitate the sale of Toys "R" Us to a group of investors in 2005 for three times what it had been worth when he took over. He had been a classic Thinker, not particularly inclined to take risks—until in his mid-thirties he took a big one, the right one, and it worked out, which permanently changed his disposition.

Learning to broaden our focus is critical to staying employed and is a practice that Thinkers in particular will want to adopt.

Truly successful people have the ability to direct their attention and focus—zooming in and out in their awareness of circumstances around them. Robert A. Bjork, the director of UCLA's Bjork Learning and Forgetting Lab, has spent a lot of time trying to understand the benefits of different approaches to learning and has found that conventional rote instruction and "learning by the book" approaches are not optimal. Bjork's research suggests that a kind of cross-training that cognitive scientists call "interleaving," where people concentrate on different concepts at different times, studying a subject closely but then moving away and returning to the first subject later, heightens long-term recall. In other words, multiple study sessions are better than single marathon cram sessions. Anyone who has experienced that moment of clarity on a run or in the shower after a day of intense concentration understands the benefit of changing perspectives and environments in problem solving.

It's a mind-set that isn't a natural habit and routine for Thinkers. They need to remind themselves to get out of their mental and behavioral ruts—or at least to look up and try to examine clearly what the terrain beyond the rut looks like.

Thinker Risk Practice Tool Kit:

- Get out of the office.
- Update your résumé.
- Create a marketing plan for yourself.
- Learn something new.
- Learn to turn off.

Tap Into Your Creativity

Creativity, an essential component in finding your way in the constantly morphing new workplace, requires what's known as "divergent thinking," the perpetual generation of fresh ideas, *combined* with "*convergent* thinking," culling and channeling those ideas into practical solutions.

Imagine sitting outside at dusk with both a microscope and a telescope. There are several "realities" available. What you are able to observe with your naked eye (grass, trees, twilight) and other senses (breeze, temperature, humidity, fragrance, birdsong); what you can see with the telescope (stars, planets, the surface of the moon); and what you can see with the microscope (the cellular structure of a blade of grass, the little hairs on an ant's back).

This same kind of near/far, micro/macro situation exists in the workplace. And too often Thinkers become so caught up in the foreground—the presentation *this afternoon,* the budget meeting *tomorrow,* the inventory report *next week*—that they fail to maintain an awareness of the big picture—new competitors, obsolete technology, stale ideas, fresh opportunities coming over the horizon. Thinkers need to consciously develop the flexibility to loosely pay attention to a variety of things on the job: from the momentary disaster of a computer crashing without the work being backed up, to a more generalized anxiety about one's ability to finish a project, to the human relationships among one's team, to the financial and broader economic issues that challenge one's organization and industry. It is often in the shifting between blue-sky contemplation and practical hands-on logistics that Thinkers gain the space to identify risks worth taking.

> *Creativity is just connecting things.*
>
> **—STEVE JOBS**

Steve Jobs understood this. "Creativity is just connecting things," he said in a *Wired* piece in 1995, just before his triumphant return to Apple. "When you ask creative people how they did something, they feel a little guilty because they didn't really *do* it, they just *saw* something. It seemed obvious to them after a while. That's because they were able to connect experiences they've had and synthesize new things. . . . A lot of people in our industry haven't had very diverse experiences. So they don't have enough dots to connect, and they end up with very linear solutions without a broad perspective on the problem. The broader one's understanding of the human experience, the better design we will have."

There is no question that developing the ability to practice elastic focus would help the Thinkers who wish they knew how to take more risks at work—39 percent of them—figure out how to do so. Have a plan, but develop an ability to improvise as the situation inevitably changes.

ELASTIC FOCUS IN PRACTICE

Effective Risk-Taking = Analysis + Trial & Error

Given Thinkers' bias for process, hard work, and deliberation, they may feel it's necessary to have a fully articulated plan before taking *any* action. But I think David Kelley, the cofounder of the successful global design and strategy firm IDEO, has an insight that is highly relevant. "Enlightened trial and error," he says, "outperforms the planning of flawless intellects." What exactly does he mean by this?

My eldest daughter's experience as she's begun her working life offers a good example of how Thinkers can benefit from learning to experiment within their field.

From the time Kate could talk she was *very* focused on food, the kind of person who asked, "What's for dinner?" at breakfast and "What's for breakfast?" at dinner. A classic Thinker who knows what she wants and then figures out through careful research and deliberation exactly what's required to get from Point A to Point B, she was focused on food from the beginning. That she happened to come of age as America at large became food obsessed was good timing for her in terms of job opportunities. During college, she indulged her passion for all things culinary in a blog she wrote for *The Atlantic* about the challenges of cooking for roommates, which serendipitously led to her first postcollege job. An editor at a major food-media company had followed her *Atlantic* blog and when Kate graduated recruited her for a full-time freelance job managing content for the company's websites. It was stressful work, benefits free, and not terribly creative, but it was in New York City, directly in her professional interest zone, and paid well, so Kate, unlike so many of her peers entering the job market at the depths of the Great Recession, could live the life of a well-employed young urban professional. Her contract kept getting renewed every three months, which in the shaky economy of recent years was a big deal. Regrettably, it was also a job with practically no management feedback and no apparent room for growth. In 2012, she exceeded the two-year limit for full-time freelancers, and when her contract was not renewed (in all likelihood because it was cheaper for her employer to train a new freelancer than to put Kate on staff and pay benefits), it was time for her to figure out what to do next.

> *The great thing about taking big chances when you're younger is you have less to lose, and you don't know as much. So you take big swings.*
>
> **—AMY POEHLER**

I suggested that she put together a list of *all* the ways she might pursue work—either directly in the food industry or in writing about food. It forced her to think both broadly and narrowly, that divergent and convergent thinking I mentioned earlier, about food as a career path. Her resulting list was broad in the sense that she cast a wide net, exploring a range of both possible writing and editing jobs—at a magazine, at a company that published cookbooks, as a blogger on her own site or for others—as well as jobs in the restaurant and larger food business. But it was narrow in the sense that she also had to assess specific companies and find out what kinds of training and experience were required to land a specific job. Which forced her to think practically about the various hurdles she'd have to surmount.

Here's how she approached the assignment.

Field: Writing/Editing

- **POSITION: Food/Travel Writer**
  REQUIREMENTS: No obvious ones—skill and experience
  FINANCES: Would depend on how I approached it—as freelance vs. salaried
  OBSTACLES: Finding a publication I want to work at and getting a job there

- **POSITION: Editor**
  REQUIREMENTS: A copyediting certification course
  FINANCES: Deciding freelance vs. salaried employment
  OBSTACLES: If freelance, finding clients; if full-time, finding a publication/company where I want to work and getting the job

- **POSITION:** Blogger

  REQUIREMENTS: Maybe in website design/HTML-type stuff

  FINANCES: Not likely to be a big breadwinner, so would need to supplement with other paying work

  OBSTACLES: Similar issues as with other writing—do I have something to say, a viewpoint people would be interested in, etc.

Field: Food Industry

- **POSITION:** Small-Business Owner

  REQUIREMENTS: I would want to take cooking classes—there's a lot of technique and practice and across-the-board experience I don't have

  FINANCES: Most likely would need to have a part-time job to get experience, although ideally would be enough to support me once I got going

  OBSTACLES: Choosing the business (what am I making, selling?) and launching/running it!

- **POSITION:** Personal Chef/Restaurant Cook

  REQUIREMENTS: I'd definitely have to go to cooking school, not just take a few classes—especially for the first, where accreditation would go a long way in recommending me to clients

  FINANCES: Same as above, more or less—classes and getting started would require money from a part-time "day job"

OBSTACLES: Really just making it work, as above, but more dependent on finding a customer base or getting a job in a restaurant (although if I did that, what's the goal—do I want to own a restaurant?)

With the winnowed-down targets of either making food or writing/editing in food media, I gave Kate another assignment, asking her to identify a few ways she could "test-drive" both a writing job related to food *and* a gig to experience first-hand what cooking professionally might be like. This is the trial-and-error part of what David Kelley was talking about.

First she researched the various New York City–based educational options that could work for her. For cooking, she found a two-night-a-week course at the Culinary Institute of America in Manhattan that would allow her to keep her part-time day jobs, but the $8,200 tuition was significant—she had to decide how she'd pay for the course and if the investment would ultimately be worth it and sufficiently on target with her possible food industry paths to warrant it. And for writing, she found a range of courses offered by several universities in New York. But before she committed herself to an intensive and expensive course of study, she decided to see if she could further distill her thinking by experiencing firsthand what it was like to work in a professional kitchen.

Through the website GoodFoodJobs.com, she found a listing for a line-cook position at a small Manhattan restaurant that didn't require previous restaurant experience—*check!*—and emphasized the restaurant's commitment both to seasonal local food—*check!*—and to finding the right person for the team rather than simply the most skilled one—another *check!* It seemed like an ideal fit for helping Kate figure out, with a minimal investment of time, whether being a restaurant line cook was something she wanted to pursue. She applied for the job and was asked to show up the next day at three p.m., to bring her knife and hat, and to wear comfortable shoes. Right away, Kate was challenged. Since she wasn't a chef, she needed to pull her best knife from her hodgepodge collection at home and buy a hat that would pass for a toque. "It was one of the most anxiety-inducing things I've ever done," she says. "I was going in knowing I was totally unprepared to be thrown into a full-on dinner service." A situation like this is a Thinker's nightmare. But she persevered.

When she showed up, she was momentarily relieved. The restaurant was small. And the chef seemed nice. "But that lasted all of three seconds," she says, "before I was told to go change and join the service." She was handed bunches of arugula and frisée, which she was instructed to inspect and choose only the finest, unbroken leaves to wash; told to prep and clean pounds of crawfish; to dice celery and carrots; and to fetch pans and pails and buckets and "more of this or more of that" from the walk-in fridge. It was a frenzy, and Kate felt as if she were doing everything wrong—not a role play-by-the-rules Thinkers are comfortable inhabiting. "I was trundling up and down a tiny set of stairs in what turned out to be wholly inappropriate gear—my worn-out sneakers instead of Crocs like everyone else, and a way-too-warm beanie instead of an actual chef's hat . . . *and* I'd tied my apron incorrectly." The whole time, too, Kate was hearing from the almost entirely male cooking staff about how terrible it was to work as a cook. And this was all before dinner had started.

During the dinner service, she was assigned to work at "the cold station," assembling salads, cheese plates, pickled eggs, and so on. Her night in the kitchen, she says, was simultaneously the most intense and the most boring ten hours of her life. First she had to learn the patois—monosyllabic commands-cum-warnings such as "behind," "beneath," and "hot." And then, "It was a constant flow of filling orders, making sure dishes were clean and out on time and plated correctly and that salads were seasoned just so . . . broken by periods of complete inactivity during which I had to clean the already spotless station just to look busy." The food, at least, was gorgeous and delicious. "Assembling a beet salad with a delicately balanced circle of greens and a gently poached egg with foam earned me compliments from the sous chef I was working with—that was the highlight of my night. Forgetting to shake the squeeze bottle of salad dressing, and watching the same cook get reamed by the chef for my mistake was one of the lowlights." She didn't even realize it was after midnight when they began the breakdown and cleanup phase.

After "the 'family meal' and a beer," she hung around, awkwardly, not knowing what more was expected of her. Eventually the chef found her, took her to his tiny office nestled among the racks of the basement kitchen, and asked her what she'd thought of the night. She said that it was challenging but exciting, a great experience for her. "He hemmed and hawed, and I knew what he wanted to say but wouldn't." So she told him that if he felt she wasn't right for them—that she was too inexperienced or not fast enough—she understood, but that she'd appreciated the opportunity. Kate was frustrated that he wasn't more direct. He only smiled and conceded that she did seem a bit out of her depth—but that she could come back, do the same intense work every night for the next two or three weeks, for no pay, and at the end, if her speed improved, he'd consider hiring her. Kate thanked him and left, "knowing already that there was *no way* this would happen."

She walked to the subway with two of the cooks, who told her more stories about what a miserable life it was. Which isn't to say they were aggressive or rude; they were incredibly friendly and gave her great advice about things to keep in mind as she considered a food service career.

Learn from Experience

"It was a thoroughly unpleasant experience," Kate says, "that I would never be able to do for a living. I'm in no way the kind of person who gets better from constant fear of failure, who tolerates needless yelling and shaming, who is comfortable having no free time, no friends, earning very little money only to be working toward becoming a person who switches from being yelled at to the one doing the yelling. It *was* a great opportunity, because it taught me a very valuable lesson—I love food, I love people who love food, but I know myself and I know that I really *could not work* in a standard restaurant kitchen, as much as I might wish I could." In other words, the one-night experiment dramatically helped her refine her focus.

By going out on a limb and test-driving the idea of working

in a restaurant kitchen, Kate gained critical insight into what she wanted from her working life. Although she's a seriously skilled and ambitious cook, she was able to check one employment subcategory off her list. This is an important skill that Thinkers need to put into practice: dipping a toe in and trying out options before investing too much time in research or study. (And for the opposite reasons Pioneers need to do this as well—to test-drive the awesome-looking car before impulsively buying it.)

Discovering she didn't want to be a line cook didn't mean that Kate stopped thinking about ways to continue to learn about a career that involved food. She did some freelance work catering dinner parties, and she heard through friends that the website *Serious Eats* was looking for a new contributing pizza editor—a perfect way to blend her desire to continue to work in the food space and work as a writer. She applied for the job and landed it. And today, after writing for *Serious Eats* and continuing another part-time job in media for a year, she's become the first full-time editorial director for an exciting and well-funded food start-up, Farmigo.com—a Web-based business linking farmers and artisanal purveyors with communities of local customers.

Beginner's Mind

A plurality of Americans, nearly half, fall into the Thinker category. The odds are that if you're reading this book, you're one. Someone who has worked hard, someone who might be feeling underappreciated for that hard work, someone who just doesn't see much growth in his or her current job. And with the unrelenting pace of most jobs today, you may also be exhausted by the prospect of trying to figure out what to do next.

Too much focus, like that of the straight-A student who's forgotten how to have fun, can keep Thinkers from dreaming of something new—and in our survey, 64 percent of them wish they could take more risks professionally. Thinkers can become rigid in their appetite for and adherence to "this is the way it's done" protocols and formulaic in their thinking.

> *In the beginner's mind there are many possibilities.*
> **—SHUNRYU SUZUKI, ZEN MASTER**

There are no easy answers in the game of career navigation and reinvention. Thinkers tend to stick to one path, but these days finding one's way through the workplace is more like 3-D chess than checkers. One of the key tools in the Thinkers' kit for learning how to embrace risk-taking is to try to recapture what they felt when they originally chose the career they have since pursued so studiously. They need to find their beginner's mind anew. Although I'm not a Buddhist, the Zen Buddhist concept of "beginner's mind" is one in which I absolutely believe: "In the beginner's mind there are many possibilities," the Zen master Shunryu Suzuki explained, "but in the expert's there are few." We don't have to try to be Steve Jobs. Lord knows I'm not. But what we all can do, like my daughter Kate, is cultivate our native curiosity about things adjacent to the work we do now. Curiosity can be nurtured, by learning to range widely, hunting and gathering ideas, skills, and people. Actor Hugh Laurie, famous for his portrayal of the curmudgeonly Dr. Gregory House, put it brilliantly: "It's a terrible thing, I think, in life to wait until you're ready. I have this feeling now that actually no one is ever ready to do anything. There's almost no such thing as ready. There's only now. And you may as well do it now. I mean, I say that confidently as if I'm about to go bungee jumping or something—I'm not. I'm not a crazed risk taker. But I do think that, generally speaking, now is as good a time as any."

Jim Cramer

Jim Cramer is host of **CNBC's** daily *Mad Money,* featuring interviews with businesspeople, viewer calls, and, most memorably, Cramer's emphatic and un-varnished opinions of particular stocks and the markets generally. He also regu-larly coanchors **CNBC's** *Squawk on the Street* and founded *TheStreet*.com, the nineteen-year-old multimedia provider of financial information and commen-tary.

Before he was a media figure, he worked in finance, most successfully at the hedge fund he founded and managed from 1987 until 2001. And before attending Harvard Law School and before his career on Wall Street, he was a journalist—a reporter for the *Tallahassee Democrat* and the *Los Angeles Herald Examiner.*

What's the most significant risk you've taken professionally?

JIM CRAMER: You want risk? Walk away from a job that you worked years to get, walk away from a job that paid you more your first month than you had made your whole life. Walk away from Goldman Sachs. Yet that's what I did [at age thirty-two] in February of 1987 because I always wanted to work for myself, and even though I loved the place, I knew that if I didn't make a move, I might never do so.

I'd first tried to get a job at Goldman in 1981, the year I enrolled in Harvard Law School. I loved the stock market, and while I wanted to be a prosecutor, I knew that the summer between your first and your second year at law school tended not to lead to where you ultimately worked. I figured if you want to go to work in stocks, you might as well go for Goldman Sachs, the best there was and the best there still is.

There was a huge problem, though. They didn't want law school kids. They wanted business school students. So I began what amounted to a two-year odyssey to prove that I deserved a slot, one of the coveted twenty-five or so positions that they granted to those who graduated business school every year. In the next two years, I interviewed with Goldman Sachs and got turned down three times and simply didn't take no for an answer. And when I finally got hired for securities sales, advising "high-net-worth individuals" and smaller institutions on what to do with their money, I couldn't believe my good fortune. The payoff was immediate, the commissions bountiful, the people terrific, the excitement nonstop.

Yet somehow, it wasn't enough. Somehow I wanted to work for myself. So I made the most stupid and the most brilliant move of my life: I quit. Four years into it, I walked away to start my own hedge fund.

Stupid? Yes, because two months after I started I was already down 10 percent for the year. I had lost almost everything I had made in the time I worked at Goldman. Then, after clawing back to plus 3 percent, I ran smack into the 1987 crash. Fortunately, I had been able to cash out ahead of it, one of those moves that in hindsight looks like genius but at the time was just total self-preservation because the market before the crash had been horrendous.

And that's where the brilliant came in. Because I had cashed out ahead of the crash, I managed to have a positive return [for the year], something that almost no hedge fund manager was able to claim. In fact, almost everyone else I knew who struck out on his own to run a hedge fund during that period ended up blown to bits.

That meant [investments of] tens of millions of dollars came my way to manage. Fortunately, I got back in close to the bottom, and I managed to rack up a return of 24 percent after all fees over a fourteen-year period—and then retired to move on to full-time writing and television.

When I look back at what I did, I still can't believe that I took that risk. But my goal had always been to work for myself, and when I had enough capital to make a go of it, I jumped at the chance. Even as it was catastrophic at first, I would do it over again in a heartbeat.

But—and this is a big but—I was single at the time, I had no kids, I wasn't fearful. I didn't have responsibilities beyond my own rental apartment and a [summer] share in a [rental] in the Hamptons. So while it was the riskiest move I ever made in my professional life, I knew I did have the rest of life to make it back if I failed.

Looking back twenty-five years later, that's certainly not the case anymore.

Chapter 4

DEFENDERS

Debbie Slater *loves* her job. She has been an executive assistant in several different companies for the whole thirty-five years of her working life. She is old-school in the best sense. Matthew Weiner could have based one of the female characters in *Mad Men* on Debbie—uncomplaining, resourceful, competent, alert to the moods of everyone in the organization, the kind of assistant who anticipates a boss's needs preemptively.

Debbie didn't dream of being a secretary, as they were still called in the 1970s. But as part of the first large wave of women entering the workforce and uncertain about what to do after graduating from a Massachusetts junior college, she followed her father's advice to "take a secretarial program to learn skills that I could take into the 'real world.'" She temped for a variety of firms until her agency was able to generate a lucrative commission landing her a permanent job as an assistant at an institutional money management firm. However, it became a lesson in learning the kind of work and workplace she *didn't* like. "It was a 'man's world,'" she says, "where they had a one-track focus—to make money, money, money. And they lacked heart and soul about people. The work was utterly dry and boring."

And she was underpaid. She sucked it up for a few years—it *was* her first real job—but eventually "I became very angry and frustrated over my salary and pushed back at my boss." Who didn't like her perceived insubordination and promptly fired her. "An hour later I was out the door. It was shocking."

Debbie's first big career risk—leaning in, as we might say today, for fair pay—didn't turn out quite the way she'd imagined, but summoning her courage was an important turning point in her working life. She had taken the first step toward deciding to align her values with her workplace.

Defenders make the country run. They are the contractors, accountants, middle managers, administrators, and clerical workers who ensure that forms get filled and filed, budgets get made, and timetables are met—that the job gets *done*. Two things matter more than anything for Defenders in a job: to work for an organization where they feel their work is valued and at a place where the employees are treated with respect. Defenders tend to be *people* people. Debbie describes herself as "a caretaker, a nurturer. As a six-year-old, when asked what I wanted to be when I grew up, I said a nurse. I gain real satisfaction knowing I've been helpful to xyz person. When I answer the phone," she says, "I'm a fabulous screener—I have a sixth sense and can tell who someone is by how they deliver the message. It's in their voice, tone, cadence, and affect. And if I doubt someone is legit, I'll grill them and have no compunction dismissing them." It helps her "guard the fort." And it's a perfect executive assistant skill that has served her well and has been much appreciated by her bosses. "When I meet someone, I get their vibe, and I can tell what they're about at a deeper level." Several years ago, the firm for which she was working at the time hired a consultant. Debbie went to her boss, the CEO, "and I said, 'You're not going to like him.' I warned him that this guy was not right for us. He hired him anyway, and then had to fire him for not delivering. To me, it was blatantly obvious from the get-go."

In our survey, Defenders were the least likely to make jokes at the expense of others. They don't really like working alone and more than any of the groups enjoy the company of their colleagues. Rather than aspiring to be the leader, Defenders value their role in helping co-workers shine. Which is something at which Debbie excels.

Debbie's next position was an even worse emotional match, working for a "rude SOB at Lehman Brothers, who had a nasty reputation and no scruples, either. The man was just awful, and they had to go outside the firm to find him an assistant—*moi*," she says, "because no internal assistant was willing to take him on, even though it would have meant a promotion. His reputation was putrid." But again, the experience was valuable. Debbie came to understand even more compellingly how essential it was for her to like and respect her boss, for both her happiness and her job performance. In fact, Debbie adds, "for me to be engaged in my work, it must be a labor of love, then my natural inclination to defend and protect my boss kicks in."

She quit, vowing to look outside of finance for her next position. For the next six years she worked in a variety of assistant positions in different fields, including real estate management and a personnel agency. With each change she acquired insight into her strengths—learning to capitalize on a core competency she shares with other Defenders: empathy.

As Debbie gained more self-knowledge through her different job experiences, she came to realize that a four-year-college degree was crucial if she was to find a position she loved. She graduated with distinction from Pace University in 1976. It was extremely risky for her to pause her embryonic career and go back to school full-time, but the degree paid off. "I still went back to administrative positions, except I was seen differently," she says. "Now I was an *executive* secretary."

The real benefit of that shift became clear in 1988, in her late thirties, when she landed a job working at *Time* magazine. Through fifteen years of trial and error, with lots of losses in the win/lose column of risks, she'd finally found her tribe. *"Time,"* she says, "was the most highly regarded newsmagazine in the world. I related to the fact that it was a *human* thing in motion all the time. News was always changing, and I loved being part of what was relevant and exciting." It energized her. "I loved the people I worked with, respected their opinions, and always found myself learning and expanding my world intellectually. I made many friends, which made my every day more meaningful." But most important, Debbie "was seen, taken seriously—including my name on the masthead—and it resonated with who I am."

By embracing the tenets of regular risk-taking, small and large—speaking up for herself, quitting boorish bosses, going back to college, sticking her neck out to help others—Debbie regularly pushed herself beyond her comfortable Defender boundaries again and again, and ultimately those bets paid off. She transformed herself and grew from the submissive generic secretary of her first job into the self-directed right hand of the founder of a thriving online media company for the last eighteen years. As a Defender, she wasn't happy until she found a place she could look forward to staying at forever.

WHO IS A DEFENDER?

Hard Workers

None of the Defenders in our survey said they had *ever* played hooky from work. It's easy to overlook the value of Defenders in an era when innovation is the Holy Grail and automation increasingly replaces their functions, but when Defenders represent 31 percent of American workers, forty-eight million people, that is absurd.

Defenders work hard. Almost 80 percent say they always do their best on the job, and nearly all Defenders—94 percent, even more than Thinkers—say that they rely overwhelmingly on logic and fact when making career decisions. They need to know how things work and despise ambiguity. Defenders invest their hard-earned income in the safest-possible mutual funds, describing their overall operating strategy as "Better safe than sorry." Three-quarters of Defenders own their homes—again, the highest percentage of any of the groups—and more of them live in suburban areas.

> *The chief danger in life is that you take too many precautions.*
>
> **—ALFRED ADLER, AUSTRIAN PSYCHOLOGIST**

Cautious

Restlessness is not a Defender attribute. Defenders like regularity and routine and are great believers in maintaining the status quo. When we asked our survey respondents if, given the binary choice, they would rather have a $75,000-a-year government job with a guaranteed pension or do something more entrepreneurial with much greater upside earning potential, 85 percent of Defenders chose the first option.

All the Defenders in our survey sample say they *hate* surprises. By and large, Defenders are not natural-born risk takers. But when push comes to shove and they feel their integrity unsupported or value to an organization underrecognized, like Debbie, they can summon the will to act decisively. Among the four types, Defenders are the least likely to travel, eat new foods, gamble, or even go on scary rides at amusement parks. For Defenders, maintaining order is everything. They tend not to be excessively unhappy in their work—indeed, Defenders' overall contentment is highly contingent on feeling connected to their work—and they don't make waves on the job. To a

Pioneer, a Defender might look unambitious and "stuck," but Defenders themselves don't see it that way and feel no urge to explore other options. For them, the grass is not always greener; when they find a turf the right shade for them, they *stay*.

Defender Strengths:
- Organizers.
- Steady.
- Put others' needs first.
- Loyal.
- Empathetic.

HOW DO DEFENDERS GET STUCK?

Head in the Sand

Defenders often allow present-moment good-enough satisfaction—what some would call complacency—to override any impulse to consider change. *All* of the Defenders in our sample say they don't like to "live on the edge." They want work and life to be predictable. This overriding desire may cause them to indulge in career wishfulness—a shockingly high 95 percent of Defenders believe that the organizations they're working for today will still exist in a decade. It's this thinking, not just risk-averse but risk-*denying*—ostriches with heads in the sand, whistling past the graveyard, pick your metaphor—that is getting Defenders into trouble when it comes to twenty-first-century work and careers.

Their sense of job security doesn't mean that some Defenders aren't worried. They know that government work, a classic Defender occupation, is no longer safe—between 2010 and 2012, jobs in U.S. state and local government fell by 450,000 and local teaching and other school jobs by 226,000. Defenders are concerned that their hours will be reduced, that their jobs will become more stressful, and that if they were to be fired, it would difficult for them to find new work.

But these worries don't seem to rise to a motivating level of action. If a Pioneer's stereotypical response to a new opportunity is "Just do it" and a Thinker's is "Mmm . . . maybe," a stuck Defender would "Just say no."

Just as narrow focus can blind a Thinker to opportunity, a Defender's dislike of uncertainty and novelty reflects several psychologically ingrained phenomena that can leave any of us—but change-resistant Defenders in particular—exposed and vulnerable to the quaking landscape of work today.

> *Uncertainty is an uncomfortable position. But certainty is an absurd one.*
>
> **—VOLTAIRE**

Complacency

Peter's story illustrates how acts of omission at work can be as damaging as acts of commission. Inaction in this climate of accelerating change, in fact, may be the greatest and most common risk of all, a risk that *feels* the opposite of risky.

Peter is a certain kind of Defender employee who's present

in every workplace: good enough at his job to keep doing it when business is good, but not exceptional enough to have been promoted or to have established a reputation as indispensable that would protect him from being laid off during leaner times. Being good enough is simply no longer the safe bet it was in the twentieth century.

Peter spent ten years working in the art department at a glossy magazine until a new boss brought in to revamp the publication promptly fired him. In his early thirties Peter had no idea how to find a new job. And when I spoke with him months after he'd been fired, he wasn't even willing to consider any job that wasn't pretty much identical to his previous one.

Having worked in one department of one division at one company for so many years, Peter doomed himself by his unwillingness to stick his neck out even a bit. During his decade at the magazine, he'd gotten to know the other people who worked in his department, and the freelancers with whom he'd forged good relationships, but beyond that he barely knew the editorial team, let alone people who worked in other magazines at the larger company. He'd developed no relationships with the broader community of art directors and editors, had joined no industry organizations, and had never had lunch with a single person with or for whom he might work in the future. It probably felt safe. The company was privately owned and profitable. As the magazine industry shrank and consolidated, he survived myriad layoffs and thought, at his midmanagement level and with his time at the company, that he was protected from being fired. But aside from federal judges and tenured professors (less than 20 percent of all college teachers), there really is no secure position in twenty-first-century working America.

Peter was not the first to see a business he'd grown up in and assumed he'd retire from transformed seemingly overnight. Nor was he the first who failed to see the transformation as a threat to *him,* an impetus to rethink, plan for contingencies, change course. Consider the transformations of the last fifteen years. The music industry upheavals caused by Napster, iPod, iTunes, Pandora, and Spotify and the impacts of cable TV, the Web, DVRs, and Netflix on every media sector. The force with which Amazon and electronic publishing have changed the business of publishing. The previously unthinkable bankruptcies and mergers and shrinkages in the airline and auto industries and every middleman business from travel agencies to real estate brokerages. Whole sectors of the economy have been disrupted dramatically by technology, turning millions of people from confident and complacent at the turn of this century to dazed and confused about how to respond today.

> *You cannot swim for new horizons until you have courage to lose sight of the shore.*
>
> **—WILLIAM FAULKNER**

When she was let go after a successful twenty-five-year career in the media industry, one very senior fifty-year-old creative executive told me that "after being a good girl my entire life, always doing the extra-credit assignments, this was not the news I was expecting. I was devastated." She confessed that she'd chosen to "ignore" the signals she had been getting from management and had failed to properly "*proactively* manage the transition into the digital era." As she put it, "Operating in my comfort zone felt safe and far preferable to thinking about striking off in some unfamiliar or untested new direction."

Changing technology isn't the only reason for uncertainty: Public sector jobs, traditional corporations, law firms, all of the places where Defenders work the most comfortably, are no longer the low-risk glide paths they seemed even a decade ago. In the absence of clarity about how the next new business model or merger or competitor or regulatory change or economic downturn will alter one's business fundamentals, the salient question is no longer: What's the least I can do to keep this job? All of us—and especially Defenders—must think in terms of not just *this job* but *a career,* understanding that change has become inevitable and that all fields are churning much more quickly—shortened product life cycles, accelerated timetables, global competition, innovation bombs everywhere.

Peter had allowed his dislike of the new and his fear of the uncharted to blunt his curiosity about how other people and other organizations in his field operate. This was a mistake for him, as it is for everyone in today's perma-flux economy. He should have dared to ask someone he didn't know at work to have a cup of coffee, or picked up the phone to set up an appointment with an editor at a magazine whose work he admired, or taken a writer whose article he'd designed out for a drink. Such outreach could have had two potential effects: making him seem like a plugged-in and integral contributor to the success of his magazine, whom the new boss might therefore have kept on, *and* preparing him for the eventuality of needing a new job. Peter had lowballed and diligently coasted his way out of a good position by allowing himself to be passive and motivated by how he might not fail, rather than by how he might succeed.

> *The truth you believe and cling to makes you unavailable to hear anything new.*
>
> **—PEMA CHÖDRÖN, TIBETAN BUDDHIST**

Defenders like Peter avoid taking risks out of what can be a willful obliviousness about how best to respond to tumultuous changes affecting their jobs. They might take action if the situation clarifies, but until then they tread water. For Peter, the situation clarified only when he found himself drowning.

WHY WE AVOID RISK

Several different but overlapping behavioral dynamics can push naturally risk-averse Defenders into the danger zone.

Fixed Mind-Set

Defenders tend to avoid anything that feels or looks like risk-taking, manifesting behavior that psychologist John Atkinson first identified in the 1960s as "failure avoidance"—the habit of lowballing expectations in order to play it safe. More recently, Stanford University psychology professor Carol Dweck has studied motivation and achievement and found that people fall into one or two basic motivational types: Either they are "fixed" in how they view their potential for achievement or they are primed for "growth."

Growth mind-set people may not always seek to be challenged, but they believe in their ability to learn and change when necessary. Fixed mind-set people, like most Defenders, believe that they came into adulthood with a certain set of skills that they are unlikely to improve upon and thus tend to gravitate to the kinds of jobs where they are rarely challenged in big ways.

Growth-oriented people—which is to say, people who regularly embrace small risks, what I'm arguing that the Thinker-plus-Defender majority of Americans must seek to become—look for ways to improve their knowledge and skills and expand their horizons. Fixed mind-set people tend to put on blinders, settle into one narrow line of work, and stick to it. And as we discovered from so many of the Defenders whom we surveyed and I interviewed, they are *content* in this approach—until their sense of security is suddenly removed, they are cast adrift, and only then realize, Uh-oh, they don't know how to swim.

Loss and Risk Aversion

It's human nature to try to cling to what we have, and Peter's just-do-nothing way of handling an unsettled working situation illustrates a concept that behavioral economists call "risk aversion." Risk aversion basically means that when we are faced with uncertainty and ambiguity about what to do next, if the threat doesn't feel acute and unavoidable, we do our best to avoid it and meanwhile try as best we can to reduce our *sense* of uncertainty.

Risk aversion is a deep evolutionary trait that has protected the species from taking frivolous or extreme risks—risks where the potential rewards aren't worth it.

Risk aversion is a close cousin of another phenomenon called "loss aversion," which refers to the nearly universal psychological predisposition to believe that the pain we'll experience in giving something up will exceed the pleasure of getting something we don't currently have. It's incredibly hard to abandon the status quo, particularly for Defenders, of a long-time job when the alternative, even an attractive-looking one, has the fundamental disadvantage of being unfamiliar territory full of unfamiliar people. Many of us prefer continuity over change. And those most determinedly geared that way are the 31 percent of us whom I call Defenders.

Defender Weaknesses:
- Fixed mind-set.
- Risk-averse.

- Too reliant on logic.
- Fear the unfamiliar.

It's the old bird-in-hand problem—the proverb instructs us never to give up the one for the *possibility* of two, to stick with the okay over the prospectively better. A 2005 George Washington University study asked a group if they were "more concerned with the opportunity to make money in the future, or the stability of knowing that your present sources of income are protected." One might think that back before the Wall Street meltdown and Great Recession, at the height of the long economic boom, when we'd convinced ourselves that financial risk was virtually obsolete, most people would have chosen the opportunity for more money—but 62 percent opted for stability.

The Sunk-Cost Fallacy

Having spent more than a decade in his good job, Peter exhibited an ongoing disinclination to consider doing anything else, which relates to a concept known as "the sunk-cost fallacy"—the notion that a lot of time or money invested in an endeavor somehow demands that *more* must be invested in exactly the same place. He had spent years toiling away, earning his place in his company's hierarchy—how could any other organization, let alone some different sort of job, give him an adequate return on that investment? We all fall victim to this kind of thinking. It's not such a big deal when we decide to sit through a movie we don't like because we've paid for the ticket; the opportunity cost (money and time spent enduring the unpleasant experience versus what might be enjoyed alternatively) isn't very great—two hours of "wasted" time and $12. But when we spend years doing work that isn't wholly gratifying, the costs are quite different. However, as Daniel Kahneman writes, the "sunk-cost fallacy keeps people for too long in poor jobs, unhappy marriages, and unpromising research projects." There's evidence that when we make ourselves aware of this tendency, we can learn to walk away and move on sooner.

Anticipated Regret

Anticipated regret is a slippery emotion that can get in the way of change—particularly for the cautious Defenders, whose loathing of surprise can make them excessively anxious when thinking about change. Lots of us worry about all of the downside "what ifs" when thinking of doing something different for a living, because we're wired to resist exchanging something we've already got in our possession for the chance that something we don't currently have might be marginally better. Imagine, then, how much harder it is for the better-safe-than-sorry Defenders to think about something as drastic as leaving what seems to be a secure job. Forty percent of Defenders in our survey say they'd *never once* made a risky career move.

> *You are what you settle for.*
>
> —JANIS JOPLIN

Defenders are right in these uncertain times to ask themselves the worst-case questions: What if I can't find work again? What if I quit my job and my spouse won't step up? What if I hate the new job? Or my new colleagues? Or I'm no good at the new work? But for Defenders this can cause a kind of paralysis. Instead of only running these worst-case hypotheticals, Defenders should listen for clear signals—that things are changing, like the arrival of new management or a boss—and come up with a plan for action.

Regret is a powerful emotion, especially when we feel we haven't taken the kinds of risks we should have to live the lives we'd imagined for ourselves or believe we deserve. We choose the cautious path, only to end up with a nagging sense of should'ves and could'ves, of opportunities lost, of yearning for second chances. Abraham Maslow, the twentieth-century psychologist who studied what enables people to achieve their full potential, believed that the most "self-actualized" people were those who were most able to navigate what he saw as the dichotomy between risk and safety that motivates behavior. "Life," he wrote, "is an ongoing process of choosing between safety (out of fear and need for defense) and risk (for the sake of progress and growth). Make the growth choice a dozen times a day." Defenders often ignore or resist the choice altogether.

The truth is that almost any choice can lead to feelings of regret: *Wow, that hamburger looks so much tastier than my salad. I wish I'd gotten that coat when it was on sale. Why didn't I speak up at yesterday's meeting when Ben got all the credit for my idea?* The trick to making the best choices we can is to understand from the get-go that *regret is intrinsic to decision making*—but that if we make lots of *small* career risks, over time we'll get into the habit. And modest, measured risk-taking (speaking up in meetings, making more cold calls) begets more risk-taking (asking for a raise, delivering a company-wide presentation) that reduces generalized fear and begets greater confidence in our skills.

WHAT'S A DEFENDER TO DO?

Feel the Uncertainty, Acknowledge the Anxiety

Most of us *try* to be pragmatic and logical about career decisions—and Defenders most of all. Defenders use routine as a crutch to protect themselves from uncertainty, but it's important for them to accept that nothing is certain, in 2015 vastly less so than in 1995.

The best solutions to modern work dilemmas—*Do I stick it out until January and get my bonus, or quit now and regain my sense of self?*—are often unclear. We're terrible at predicting what will make us happy in the abstract and particularly in an abstract future. In *Stumbling on Happiness,* Harvard psychology professor Daniel Gilbert discusses the relationship between anxiety and planning. Both, he points out, are "intimately connected with thinking about the future," and since planning "requires that we peer into our futures . . . anxiety is one of the reactions we may have when we do." Defenders need to understand that anxiety, although scary, is a natural result of contemplating change, like sore muscles after a hard workout. And that decision making is not just about quantifiable outcomes, but also about listening to what we might *feel* in each scenario. In his book *Predictably Irrational*, behavioral economist Dan Ariely examined all of the factors that shape the seemingly rational decisions we make and suggests that the only way we can make optimal decisions is to "experience and understand the emotional state we will be in at the other side of the experience. Learning how to bridge this gap is essential to making . . . the important decisions in our lives."

Defender Risk Practice Tool Kit:
- Acknowledge uncertainty and anxiety.
- Value surprise.
- Create structure to help in decision making.
- Just say yes.

Choice Architecture

This strategy is something that Harvard Law professor Cass Sunstein and University of Chicago behavioral economist Richard Thaler laid out in their book, *Nudge: Improving Decisions About Health, Wealth, and Happiness.* They say that what helps people most in decision making is something they call "choice architecture," which is "a structure to help people organize the context in which they make choices."

For those of us reluctant to embrace anything out of the ordinary, we don't necessarily need to begin with huge, life-altering risks such as quitting a job or leaving a successful legal career to work at a school in Costa Rica—although after a series of smaller steps, one might ultimately end up making such a drastic swerve. What we need is a framework to guide us as we gather information and then make choices. For Defenders, the framework might be something along the lines of committing to having coffee every week or so with a person at work with whom they rarely interact or deciding to attend a lecture series on a topic that's of interest but that falls outside of the strict definition of their field. It's important for Defenders to make concrete plans to begin to shift their mind-set from keeping their head down and hanging on, toward growth and potential change. Once a strategic scaffolding is in place, it can take just a nudge—actually, a series of little nudges, which tend to get easier the more you do them.

Value Surprise: Do Something Different, Vary Routine

Careers don't operate best on cruise control. One's route through life is more apt to be like a curving mountain road than a straight-shot interstate highway. Defenders just don't want to admit it. Which is why it's easier said than done for a don't-rock-the-boat Defender to welcome the out-of-the-ordinary event that can alter one's perspective at work. Defenders need practice inviting the new into their lives. It's a mental muscle that takes time to develop. Keri Smith, author of the terrific *How to Be an Explorer of the World,* suggests five ways that I think a surprise-hating Defender can begin to get in touch with the more ineffable parts of existence: observe, collect, analyze, compare, notice patterns. In other words, *tune in* to the novelty of the new and regularly welcome it in. Does everyone at work toil away through the lunch hour? Rather than eating lunch at your desk, invite others to join you and take a break. Cultivate curiosity about how others go about their work—make a point to ask someone at work a specific question about his or her job. And do it with a different person fifty-two weeks in a row. Sit facing a different direction at your desk. Dress up and see if people treat you any differently. The point is to enlarge your experience.

Practice Being Bold

Actor Jim Carrey, the son of a hard-core Defender (and not the first source you might turn to for career advice), gave his own excellent take on this tension in a recent commencement address. "My father," he told the new graduates, "could have been a great comedian, but he didn't believe that that was possible for him, and so he made a conservative choice. Instead, he got a safe job as an accountant . . . and when I was twelve years old he lost that job. I learned many great lessons from my father, not the least of which was that you could fail at what you don't love, so you might as well take a chance on doing what you love." He went on to say that "so many of us choose our path out of fear disguised as practicality, what we really want seems impossibly out of reach and ridiculous to expect, so we never dare to ask the universe for it—I'm saying I'm the proof that you can ask the universe for it—and if it doesn't happen for you right away, it's only because the universe is so busy fulfilling my order."

Defenders, I believe, are too often driven by the fear of personal growth that Abraham Maslow (and Jim Carrey) describes. Fear of rocking the boat, fear of upsetting others, fear of not having what it takes to do something different. In order to overcome this fear, they need to practice saying yes to opportunity. A dozen years before Elizabeth Gilbert wrote her bestselling *Eat, Pray, Love* odyssey, when she was a young nobody, she decided to *go for it*. "One morning in 1993," she has written, "I walked into the offices of a famous magazine in New York City and asked for a job as a writer. I had no appointment, no experience, and not a single published article to my name. But I'd had an epiphany: Nobody was ever going to knock on my door and say, 'We understand a talented writer lives here and we'd like to help her with her career!' No. I would have to go knocking on doors." Knocking on doors is a Defender's nightmare. But as Gilbert goes on, "I just walked in off the street and asked to be hired as a reporter. And guess what? It didn't work! (Of course it didn't work; they weren't dummies, and I was totally unqualified—jeez, how do you think the world operates, people?) But I still think of it as one of the most important moments of my life because it was the boldest. When I went home that day, I was still broke and obscure, but at least I knew I was brave. I wouldn't have to suffer the pain of knowing I hadn't tried."

She knew she wouldn't have to suffer the pain of knowing she hadn't tried. Only 14 percent of Defenders think of themselves as brave. The kind of *manageable courage* Gilbert describes—the bravery of risking embarrassment, the bravery of stepping out with the knowledge that failure is possible or even probable—is something the other 86 percent of Defenders need to practice.

A CONVERSATION ON RISK:

Sheryl Sandberg

In her book *Lean In: Women, Work, and the Will to Lead*, Sheryl Sandberg, the chief operating officer of Facebook, examines the slow progress women have made in getting leadership positions. As a former Google sales executive and chief of staff to the U.S. Treasury secretary, for the last two decades she has "been at the table"—one of her commandments for women to become successful—watching what distinguishes the career trajectories of women from men.

What's the most significant risk you've taken professionally?

SHERYL SANDBERG: After I had my first child, I began to leave work at five thirty so I could get home in time to nurse. Once my son was asleep, I would jump back online and continue my workday. Still, I went to great lengths to hide my schedule and worried that if anyone [at Google] knew I was leaving the office at that time, they might assume I wasn't completely dedicated to my job. This felt extremely risky.

Once I became COO [of Facebook two years later], I wanted co-workers to know that Facebook cared more about results than face time, so I opened up at a company-wide meeting and stated that I left at five thirty. Later, this "news" became public and spread throughout the Internet. Journalist Ken Auletta joked that I could not have gotten more headlines if I "had murdered someone with an ax."

While I was glad to jump-start the discussion, all the attention gave me this weird feeling that someone was going to object and fire me. I had to reassure myself that this was absurd. Still, the clamor made me realize how hard it would be for someone in a less senior position to ask for or admit to this schedule. We have a long way to go before flextime is accepted in most workplaces. And it will only happen if we keep raising the issue.

Chapter 5

DRIFTERS

Daniel Thorson, twenty-seven, grew up in idyllic small-town America—in the village of Cazenovia, New York (population: 2,835), the son of two political scientists who teach at nearby Syracuse University. Like that of his fellow millennials, his worldview has been significantly shaped by negative events— Columbine, 9/11, the Iraq war, Katrina, the financial melt-down—as well as by the digital revolution and taken-for-granted marvels of technology. He graduated from Hobart and William Smith Colleges in 2009. His major in philosophy wasn't just a passing fancy: For him, questions of ethics and truth and right living are fundamental. But even in the best of times, philosophy is not a major guaranteed to lead to many job offers.

Entering the workforce at the nadir of the Great Recession could have discouraged Daniel, but he'd worked minimum-wage jobs all through high school and college—busing tables in restaurants, mowing lawns, painting houses, cleaning boats—so he knew he'd be able to pay the rent. Having graduated college without debt, unmarried, and childless, he decided to view his twenties as a chance for professional exploration. His optimism in the face of uncertainty and his belief in his ability to shape a working life of his choosing are traits he shares with many of his peers. The Pew Research Center has been tracking his generation and in a recent study described Daniel's cohort as "confident, self-expressive . . . upbeat and open to change."

Through a friend of his older sister, Daniel found a position "somewhere between an internship and a real job" at a Washington, D.C., environmental action nonprofit. He worked "as an indentured young person doing all the stuff that old people didn't know how to do, like social media, graphic design, and video editing." Like many people working today, he found it necessary to supplement his income with part-time work as a stock person at Borders—he was among the last hired before Borders went out of business in 2011. He loved the Borders perk of being "able to read anything I wanted," but he found his mission-oriented job at the nonprofit not what he'd expected.

"I wanted to change the world after college, and I thought this would let me do that, but I discovered that big nonprofits are just another form of bureaucracy." Daniel had gotten into meditation in college, starting a mindfulness group at his fraternity, but it was during his stint in D.C. that it became a really important part of his life. "I meditated enough to realize how unhappy I was, but I also came to realize that this would be a good time in my life to go meditate a lot. So that's what I did." He quit to live at an intensive meditation center in up-state New York.

While the Pew study found that Daniel's cohort of workers will be more likely than others to hop from job to job, dab-bling in a range of occupations in the hope of finding satisfac-tory work, Daniel's willingness to quit his not-so-bad first postcollege job was motivated specifically by something cen-tral to the Intentional Drifter. Intentional Drifters use their employment as a means of enriching a lifelong pursuit of self-discovery and creative or spiritual expression. They define work success more by their personal input than by the tangible output. And while Thinkers and Defenders tackle work issues through the diligent application of logic, Drifter actions are less obviously effortful—they tend to skim along the surface of things, responding intuitively, more through instinct.

Bartering work as a volunteer coordinator in exchange for room and board at the center, Daniel spent about one hun-dred days in silence over the course of ten months. "The expe-rience changed my life and was a really big deal."

Just as he was completing this deep dive into self-awareness in 2011, the Arab Spring movements were igniting. And then he heard through social media about this thing planned for New York City called Occupy Wall Street. Daniel was "im-mediately drawn to that" and moved to New York to become part of the cause, living mainly outside in lower Manhattan for many weeks. "Looking back," he says, "it was a pivotal point in my own development, just like meditation."

Although the movement seems to have had few lasting impacts, Daniel says he learned good work skills at Occupy. "How to work with people, how to create new processes and systems, and then how to iterate on them based on feedback, and how to lead groups and make complex decisions in high-pressure situations." He also identified something central to his emerging career philosophy: "how fun and satisfying it is to be doing work that is connected with your own sense of meaning, feeling like you were making a difference in the world. Really better than I can imagine any paycheck."

Daniel had been part of Occupy Wall Street for about seven months when he came to feel that its almost oxymoronic inherent tension—an organization of anarchists—ultimately didn't suit him. He decided to move once again. He found his way to Boulder, Colorado, and a job working as the community coordinator for Buddhist Geeks, a company founded in 2006 and dedicated to figuring out how "to serve the convergence of Buddhism with rapidly evolving technology." It was a great fit for him, allowing him to blend his meditation practice with his developing skill set of managing people and processes. And all went well until it turned out, about a year and a half into the project, that the start-up "wasn't financially sustainable—and like many projects, it just didn't end up working." Daniel was laid off.

But now, knowing lots of people in the national "Buddhist scene" allowed him to "put out a distress beacon" and land a job immediately as a project manager at a design firm in Boulder. "It was good work and well paid," he says, "but just not what I wanted to do." Today he is back on the East Coast, spending six hours a day meditating and another six hours "doing product development, website design, organizational development, and meeting facilitation" for the nonprofit Center for Mindful Learning in Burlington, Vermont.

It may appear as if Daniel is building his career in a somewhat random fashion, but that would be a dated misunderstanding. Nonlinear and opportunistic, yes, with each step along the way unknown and unclear until he takes it, but with a real sense that he's discovering and following a path, not *aimlessly* drifting. There is no particular profession or occupational brass ring in mind, but he is headed in a certain direction: He wants to earn a living by raising awareness of the benefits of contemplation and leave a light footprint on the planet. Once he decided to align his work with his values, he made the decision to live extremely frugally, often bartering his services to cover his living expenses. This strategy allows him to pursue the work he finds meaningful with less anxiety. He doesn't see any of the choices he's made so far as very risky. "For me, the much bigger and more real risk is living a boring, meaningless, unhappy, unfulfilled life—that is the real risk and danger."

Daniel says without irony that he has "*huge* ambitions, wanting to completely change the planet and the unfolding of history. All I can do is ride the wave that arises in front of me and trust that I'm building skills and learning things and doing things that are useful," he says. "I don't know what else I can do. If I try to pretend that I can control my own future, I think I'll probably just end up closing myself off to a lot of amazing opportunities." He connects what he's learned from his meditation practice with his career. "Meditation helps me see the fluidity of everything."

> *Eventually everything connects—people, ideas, objects. The quality of the connections is the key to quality per se.*
>
> **—CHARLES EAMES, AMERICAN DESIGNER**

Daniel's unorthodox, Drifter-informed notion of ambition, at once grand and modest, offers an alternate framework for defining success in an uncertain economy. Unlike the typical Pioneer, the *Intentional* Drifter is expansive, with goals that fall outside of standard titles and purely financial returns. He drifts, but he has a rudder and learns to master the ability to move in a general direction, tacking and turning responsively to the currents and winds, with a hand lightly on the tiller.

DRIFTER BY CHOICE

Drifters have often been viewed as feckless ne'er-do-wells. But the Intentional Drifter is qualitatively different. Those I've interviewed consciously *choose* to build their working lives outside of conventional twentieth-century norms. In an age of increasingly nonexistent job security, their countercultural approach begins to look sensible. For Intentional Drifters, the journey as destination isn't a lip service cliché, but the core belief that guides their approach to work and life.

Eric, sixty-three, an American who spent the last twenty-five years in Europe but recently moved back to the United States, has spent a lifetime as an Intentional Drifter. While he covers his modest living expenses doing English translation work in a variety of languages (Danish, Swedish, Norwegian, French, Portuguese) for a variety of businesses, he admits that regular full-time work holds no allure for him. He's done a lot of things: driven a taxi, delivered Amway and Avon products to local distributors, prepped in a French kitchen, been a university lecturer on literature. But in his four decades since college, he has had only one stint in a nine-to-five job, which lasted eighteen months. For him, as with Drifters in general, Intentional as well as Unintentional, a job and a paycheck are *purely* the means to an end. In his case, it's all about having the minimum necessary to pursue his passion—playing all kinds of percussion in all kinds of bands, from congas and bongos to the *caixa, surdo, chocalho, berimbau, güiro,* and *shekere.*

Eric is very clear about what matters to him. "It needs to be established up front that I do not in general equate work with what brings satisfaction. Call it my working-class and peasant heritage, but I see work as what has to be endured to pay one's way. The ideal would be as much return as possible for the least effort expended." He longs to live free of worldly expectations and obligations, "appreciating a birdsong or color, the touch and scent of one's love, the laughter one might induce in a child, the elegant movements of dancers to the rhythm one is expressing, et cetera, et cetera."

WHO ARE DRIFTERS?

March to Their Own Drummer

There have always been people out there pursuing nontraditional career paths—artists, performers, craftspeople—driven by personal ambitions that fall outside the standard "respectable" measurements of titles and income. But the dissolution of the twentieth-century American social contract regarding employment—you work reliably and loyally, and your job and its benefits are secure—has encouraged a growing fraction of Americans to conceive of entirely new approaches to their working lives. Communities all over the country, not just Brooklyn and Portland and Marfa, but Omaha and Detroit and Durham, North Carolina, are inhabited by people working in modes not seen since pre–Industrial Revolution cottage industries and guilds. The population of individual American makers and service providers who work independently—cabinetmakers, chocolatiers, designers, vintners, tutors—with no Pioneer-like desire to "scale" beyond a reasonable standard of living, is reaching a size that constitutes a new condition in the American economy. Among the four Risk/Reward types, Drifters have the highest percentage who self-identify as craftspeople.

Drifter Strengths:
- Ambition beyond making money.
- Willing to work outside of traditional environments.
- Open to possibility.
- Appreciative of the process—being here now.

Victim of Circumstance

But then there are the *Unintentional* Drifters, people who have been *cast* adrift, involuntarily unmoored from the American dream by job loss, by illness, by family circumstance, by psychological self-sabotage. They hop from job to job not only without a plan or plausible destination, but without a compass. In other words, like a rolling stone, but with none of the Bob Dylan–esque romance that Intentional Drifters bring to the "just getting by" life.

This group is the most down on their luck of all the Risk/Reward types. They feel abandoned and, as their traditional industrial base has eroded, are unsure about how to find the right skills for the new economy. Accustomed to secure and well-paid union jobs in the last century, they struggle today, working intermittently in sectors such as fast food and transportation.

The Unintentional Drifter is unmoored and uncertain. These Drifters are uncomfortable thinking critically about how to plan for something better, and they are not in touch with their intuition when it is telling them something important. The gap between what they used to have and the options they see available to them in today's marketplace undermines their confidence, resulting in a form of paralysis.

Drifter Weaknesses:
- Outdated skill sets.
- Confused.
- Lack confidence.

> *The greatest risk to man is not that he aims too*
> *high and misses, but that he aims too low and hits.*
> **—MICHELANGELO**

Karen is an Unintentional Drifter. Shocked by divorce in 2007 after twenty-five years of marriage, and being out of the workforce for a decade, Karen was suddenly faced with having to find a job. As her retirement savings and the value of her house were decimated during the Great Recession, she struggled to keep her head above water. At sixty-two, she has been a department store salesperson, a manager of a real estate development office, and a volunteer director of a gourmet food association in Colorado, but she is unsure of how to turn that into a narrative that would seem attractive to a prospective employer. Her work was always secondary to her husband's, and she never thought of herself as having a career with a design or shape—because she never imagined that she would have to. Karen is right to be worried. To find *any* work will be a challenge at sixty-two—let alone a job paying what she needs to keep living in her nice exurban Denver house. Many companies understandably feel it doesn't make economic sense to train people in their early sixties—their health care costs are higher, their skills are often out-of-date. Karen's feeling a debilitating sense of urgency "to find a job of some sort, for money, and for my mind."

Bob is yet another Unintentional Drifter. He grew up in a small town in Ohio, the son of teachers. He attended a local college in the early 1980s and, after graduating, moved—drifted—to Washington, D.C., where he worked for a few years in a series of clerical jobs before joining Amtrak as a porter.

But working life didn't turn out as Bob had hoped. In 2000, at age thirty-eight, he lost his Amtrak job and moved back home with his mother, getting a night-shift job as a quality control checker at a tire manufacturing plant—before the odd hours took their toll and he was fired. The only job he's been able to hold since then is working minimum wage as the cart wrangler at the neighborhood supermarket.

> *Without work, all life goes rotten, but when work is soulless, life stifles and dies.*
>
> **—ALBERT CAMUS**

Unintentional Drifters like Karen and Bob illustrate how people from different walks of life can find themselves struggling to get work. They lack Pioneers' vision and chutzpah, Thinkers' ambition and focus, Defenders' prudence and reliability, and Intentional Drifters' laissez-faire. They are the most affected by self-doubt and are terrified at the idea of starting over. They are the least comfortable with ambiguity of all the Risk/Reward types and the most exhausted by the multiple everyday work decisions they face. Even though many of them believe they could be trained to get a better job or career, the single largest obstacle preventing Unintentional

Drifters from pursuing their dream job is that "it just seems too difficult."

THE DRIFTER RISK PRACTICE

It's hard to know what to suggest for people in circumstances as challenging as Karen's and Bob's without seeming glib or callous. But when we asked our survey respondents about improving their work situations, they were clear about what would benefit them the most. Both Intentional and Unintentional Drifters agree that broadening their outreach—making new contacts—and upgrading and/or acquiring new skills are key to their continued employment.

Build Robust Networks of Contacts

The best thing both kinds of Drifters can do to improve their odds of happening upon the right work is to meet new and different kinds of people. Back in the late twentieth century, Stanford University sociologist Mark Granovetter studied 282 men looking for work and discovered something surprising. Most of the men found their jobs through their personal networks of contacts rather than employment agencies or help wanted listings. But more interesting, and counterintuitive, the personal contacts most "indispensable to individuals' opportunities" were *not* their closest friends *or* random people they'd just lucked into meeting. Rather, the really useful job contacts came from the in-between category—people with whom the job seekers had relatively long-term but also relatively *weak* ties, people with whom they weren't intimate but had known long enough to forge and maintain a relationship over some years. In addition, the chances of being successful in making a major job change was roughly proportional to the degree those contacts' occupations were *different* from one's own.

In today's transforming economy, Granovetter's vintage findings that mobility itself can be self-generating—people with more jobs generate more contacts, which in turn generate more potential employment opportunities—are surely even more relevant. To be clear: Contacts generate jobs, which generate contacts, which generate jobs, which generate contacts, ad infinitum, in a classic virtuous circle. Daniel Thorson, for instance, hadn't consciously "networked" but discovered the value of his loose network of contacts when he lost his job at Buddhist Geeks and was able to tap into that web to find new work. While Intentional Drifters are more naturally inclined to be open to meeting new people, it's also easy for them to become isolated in their niches—Eric meeting only fellow percussionists, Daniel only other meditators. All Drifters will benefit from widening their circles of contacts.

Life shrinks or expands in proportion to one's courage.

—ANAÏS NIN

In *Working Identity: Unconventional Strategies for Reinventing Your Career*, Herminia Ibarra, an organizational behavior professor at INSEAD, the global graduate business school, writes that people's "[existing] contacts [don't] help them reinvent themselves . . . the networks we rely on in a stable job are rarely the ones that lead us to something new and different." Drifters of both types know this but are uncertain how to put the knowledge into practice. There's a reason that most jobs suggested by headhunters or even close friends and colleagues rarely feel right when we're interested in making a forty-five- or ninety-degree career shift. Most people we know from one line of work can imagine us only doing more or less the same thing. It's people outside our accustomed network who have the distance to imagine different applications of our skills.

Intentional Drifters benefit from joining co-working spaces such as Grind. The proliferation of these spaces (in 2013, they grew by 40 percent nationwide) means that almost every mid-size or larger city will have one. They are increasingly industry specialized and with enough variety of sizes, locations, and pricing models that even impecunious and unconventional Drifters can probably find a fit that can give them a home port to establish new relationships, help them share knowledge and costs, and feel part of a community of *doers and makers.*

Unintentional Drifters can also benefit from a co-working environment, but given how prone they are to inaction in the face of doubt, they may need a more structured action plan. Unintentional Drifters should outline the ways they plan to meet people in and outside of their would-be field. A first step, for instance, might be to tap into free programs offered in their communities—in public libraries, local colleges, museums, and other not-for-profit institutions offering lectures, presentations, and exhibitions about a vast range of subjects. Unintentional Drifters should find something that piques their interest (a course in brewing beer, refinishing antiques, coding) and make a point of meeting one or two people at each event they attend. And then following up—setting up a coffee or drink to find out more about why the people they met were there. It is through low-stress social interactions like these that the Unintentional Drifter can find inspiration and even mentors to help them move into new work.

Expanding one's network of professional contacts to its fullest scope has another extremely important benefit. A wide circle of contacts exposes us to potential role models for how we might reconfigure our own careers and lives. Try to visit people where they work to get a firsthand sense of what it might be like to run a small firm, be an engineer or a veterinary assistant. "As our points of comparison shift from inside to outside our organization," Herminia Ibarra writes in *Working Identity*, "and as we encounter more and more people who have changed careers, a 'tipping point' occurs. Our actions become self-reinforcing: We start to feel more determined to make a change and seek out others who have already done so."

Practice Marketing Yourself

Meeting people at organized events gives Unintentional Drifters—people who tend to be insecure in their inability to self-market—a way to talk about themselves over and over again within an affinity group, people who self-select for a shared interest. Discussing one's work, flexing this muscle regularly, can allow a Drifter to understand through trial and error the best ways to describe his or her experience and competencies and to develop the confidence to do so.

Drifter Risk Practice Tool Kit:
- Build a broader network of contacts.
- Practice self-marketing.
- Learn new skills.
- Build resiliency.

Learn New Skills

Even those who don't need (or think they don't need) to maintain a tool kit of *current* skills would benefit from regularly brushing up. This is true for nearly everyone, from social entrepreneur to advertising copywriter to biotech researcher. Consider a seemingly old-school job like repairing cars: As automobiles have become rolling agglomerations of microchips, powered in all sorts of ways—gas, diesel, hybrid, electric—the people who repair them have to study a lot to remain employable.

That sort of ongoing professional training is now happening in all sorts of places. There's Lynda.com, an online aggregator of training videos in digitally disrupted disciplines such as graphic design and there are sixteen hundred American community colleges and sixteen thousand public libraries as well as a burgeoning DIY person-to-person training market.

The concept is not new—for most of the last century, physicians and teachers, for instance, have been required to take continuing education courses to maintain their certifications. But what is new is the accelerating rate of technological transformation, which means that nearly everyone who works must be familiar with the new tools in their fields.

And lots of skills can be rented rather than acquired. For the Drifter figuring out how to become a solopreneur, it's good to know you can subcontract and outsource work to experts. Web-based clearinghouses such as TaskRabbit and Mom Corps and Mechanical Turk and oDesk connect freelance workers with every sort of temporary and part-time job. Need an accountant? Occasional legal advice? Graphic design? Source a local employee through one of these sites. Or hire one of them to train you to do the work.

Build Emotional Resiliency

The real test with risk-taking comes with how we handle adversity. In turbulent times, the need to bolster emotional resiliency is true for all types, but particularly for the Unintentional Drifter. Resiliency is knowing how to pick yourself up when you've been flattened. In *It's Always Personal,* my book about emotion at work, I wrote about how resiliency is not so much about the *speed* of recovery from emotional assaults—such as your business failing or getting fired—as it is about the *process.* It's where you come out on the other end that allows interesting and useful growth. If you learn, you grow. The more you risk and fail, in ways large and small, the more you understand how to rebound. Failing at some attempt in one's career can be painful and miserable, but it's not actually dying—no, it's like dying in a *video game,* where you're resurrected, able to play again, savvier and wiser.

Emotional resiliency at its most basic is one's ability to respond to and *recover* from stressful situations and crises. It's our ability to bounce back after setbacks. It's like the shock absorbers on your car that let you glide over all the little bumps and potholes practically oblivious. Many Unintentional Drifters have lost or never had proper shock absorbers.

One way to build resiliency is to *objectify* one's feelings. If you cannot *name* what's bothering you, you can't find a remedy. Rather than simply *feeling* the stress, or even *thinking* about what's stressing you out, start *writing* about it. I know—it seems as though there's no big difference between thinking and writing, but University of Texas psychologist James Pennebaker has studied resiliency and stress and found that thinking alone tends to trigger unproductive rumination—obsessing about some detail over and over again—whereas writing about what we're feeling helps us organize our thoughts more effectively, enabling us to pin down what's driving the anxiety most acutely. Once you articulate the root cause of a problem—my anger over being fired is keeping me from moving forward, I'm terrified to go back to school, I'm too old to apply for that kind of a job—you begin to know how it might be fixed.

Not in his goals but in his transitions man is great.
—RALPH WALDO EMERSON

Gaining greater control of your working life and career can be as simple as making a commitment to a small daily change. Sheryl Sandberg is a powerful case study of how professional evolution or reinvention can start with modest sorts of everyday risk-taking—in her case, by doing something as seemingly minor as defining professional boundaries by leaving work at a reasonable hour. The first such positive action can empower you with a sense of personal agency that is energizing. As Ralph Waldo Emerson wrote, "Not in his goals but in his transitions man is great."

Tory Burch

Tory Burch opened a small boutique in lower Manhattan's Nolita neighborhood in 2004, and since then her brand has grown into a global fashion business with more than one hundred freestanding stores, toryburch.com, and a presence in more than one thousand department and specialty stores. She's been named Accessories Designer of the Year by the Council of Fashion Designers of America, as well as one of *Glamour*'s Women of the Year and *Forbes*'s World's Most 100 Powerful Women. In 2009, she launched the Tory Burch Foundation to support the economic empowerment of female entrepreneurs.

What's the most significant risk you've taken professionally?

TORY BURCH: The biggest professional risk I've ever taken was starting a business. The concept was for beautifully designed, well-made pieces that didn't cost a fortune. I had worked in the fashion industry for many years in marketing and PR, but I had never been a designer or a CEO. I had to learn on the job.

I was thirty-six years old and was taking some time off to be with my three young boys. I began putting together image books—[including] sketches and photographs of my parents, whose effortless elegance embodied the concept. I started working out of my apartment with a small team and traveled often to Hong Kong, where we set up a sourcing and production office.

When we needed to raise capital to get the company off the ground, I approached family and friends. It was exciting and stressful at the same time. I told people I only wanted them to invest if they were prepared to lose their money. I was willing to bet on myself, but bringing in other people raised the stakes, and I didn't want anyone to be disappointed.

With the capital we raised and a personal investment, we were able to open a retail store and launch our e-commerce site. There were many naysayers, and I didn't take what they said to heart. It was a challenge, but I didn't second-guess myself. The experience made me realize I was an ambitious person—and with that was a willingness to take risks.

Chapter 6

ALIGNING RISK WITH OUR TRUEST SELVES

Rosanne Cash seamlessly blurs the lines between country, rock, roots, and pop. She's released eleven singles that have been number one hits and has won four Grammys, three of them in 2015. A prolific author as well, she has published *Bodies of Water, Penelope Jane: A Fairy's Tale,* and her memoir, *Composed.* Her essays have appeared in *The New York Times,* the *Oxford American, New York, Newsweek,* and *Rolling Stone,* among other publications. In other words, she has habitually ventured into unfamiliar territory.

Rosanne, like many artists, says she regularly feels as if she's taking risks—small and large. "There are series of small risks in my work every day, going for a different note, improvising, trying out a new song in concert for the first time, or working with a new musician. Just walking onstage sometimes feels like a risk. I performed at the Rolling Stones tribute at Carnegie Hall [in 2012], and when they asked what song I wanted to do, I immediately said, 'Gimme Shelter,' because I've always thought it was one of the five greatest rock-and-roll songs of all time. There couldn't have been a riskier choice for me. It was thrilling."

It is thrilling to experience the upside *rush* when risks taken prove successful. Those kinds of risks, the ones where Rosanne pushes creative boundaries and puts her public identity on the line, are the fun ones for her. The less fun risks arise from the tension that exists between her desire to experiment as an artist and the homogenizing, risk-averse forces of commerce.

"In 1989," she says, describing the first of what she says have been her two greatest career risks, at age thirty-four, "I had a hugely successful album that had four number one singles on it, and I had some leverage with my label, Sony, so I asked if I could produce a record myself. I made a small, dark, acoustic record called *Interiors*. It was something of a mission statement for me. It was authentic and personal and kind of rough around the edges. I thought I had done the best work of my life. My record label heard it and said, 'We can't do anything with this.'" They put out a single but didn't do any promotion for it and clearly wanted to let the record disappear. Rosanne was devastated.

About three months after the release, Rosanne was on a plane, staring out the window, and it came to her that she had to ask to be released from the label or at least transferred from Nashville to the New York division. "I called my dad"—that was Johnny Cash—"and asked his advice, something I rarely did. He said, 'Screw 'em. You belong in New York.'" Rosanne called a meeting with the head of the label and went in alone—no manager or lawyer. She asked them to let her go. She had been there twelve years. Basically, they said, "We'll miss you," and the meeting was over in twenty minutes. "I walked out," she says, "and had to lean against the wall, I was so dizzy. I was scared I had made the biggest mistake of my life."

> *Don't become something just because someone else wants you to, or because it's easy; you won't be happy. You have to really, really, really, really, really want to do it, even if it scares the shit out of you.*
>
> **—KRISTEN WIIG**

That decision, not to surrender to her label's don't-color-outside-the-lines marketing formula, was life changing. "It was the best thing I've ever done for myself. I moved to New York in 1991, I got divorced, I met the love of my life, and that dark little record was nominated for a Grammy."

Almost without exception, every person I've interviewed for this book who successfully managed to switch jobs, change careers, or simply shift the way they've been approaching their work described the big risks they took as ones that allowed them to reconnect with some significant aspect of their essential selves—a belief, need, desire, and/or part of their sensibility—that had been ignored or suppressed or improperly harnessed. They told me that they felt reenergized and inspired with a renewed passion for work.

Understanding when, *why,* and how to take important professional risks successfully is the goal of a *regular habit* of risk. To be successful in your career, it's essential to become *conscious,* acutely aware on a day-to-day basis, of the things that give you more than just the satisfaction of a paycheck. As we know from our study of the Risk/Reward types, some people find purpose and meaning in their work by keeping things flawlessly organized, others from creating a collegial environment, others from earning a great salary, others from being the disruptive innovator. Finding satisfaction in work is highly idiosyncratic. Risking wisely doesn't mean that we reject our core identity—that a Defender, for instance, must throw natural-born caution to the wind. No, optimal risk-taking requires that we align the risks we choose to take with our truest selves. *New York Times* columnist David Brooks describes this kind of risk-taking as finding one's agency—or discovering the "solid criteria that will help [people] make their own judgments." He says, "Agency is not automatic. It has to be given birth to, with pushing and effort. It's not just the confidence and drive to act. It's having engraved inner criteria to guide action." Brooks believes that the "agency moment can happen at any age, or never." By inviting a regular habit of risk into your life, you can tip the scale in favor of the moment happening.

The risk that Rosanne Cash took when she released her left-turn album *Interiors* gave her a new and different set of bona fides in the industry. And her experience highlights another fundamental tenet central to a practice of risk: The trajectory going forward after taking a big leap isn't necessarily permanent or automatic thereafter. There's a reason the "two steps forward, one step back" adage rings so true. Change is hard and requires an acknowledgment that it will demand ongoing dedication in its pursuit.

"Things didn't go easier after that," Rosanne says. "In fact, they became much more difficult for quite some time. The divorce was excruciating, I was broke, I was the subject of a lot of vicious rumors, and I had no more chart hits after that. But my life opened up and I started relying more on my own instincts." Four years later, she took another risk when she asked to be released from the label entirely, even though her contract wasn't up, because it just didn't feel right to her. Again she went in alone, even though her manager thought that was a bad idea. "They let me go, and I started from scratch again."

Rosanne thinks of career risks like chess, in a way. "There is an element of instinct, but it's mostly logic and planning and creating a new vision for the future. The other risks, the artistic risks, are the ones that infuse my soul with inspiration and propel me forward and refine my skills and intuition. Those are the risks that connect me with my own authenticity. The career risks are a First World problem. The artistic risks make me who I am." When she "started relying more on my own instincts," she says, "my life opened up."

TUNE IN TO YOUR INNER VOICE

How *do* we learn to take the kinds of risks that infuse our souls with inspiration, propel our lives forward, and connect us with our own authenticity? Journalist Hunter Thompson and Holocaust survivor and psychiatrist Viktor Frankl—about as divergent in their life missions and experiences as it's possible to be—shared a conviction that it is through the search for significance that people ultimately find their true life's purpose. In the 1983 preface of his Auschwitz memoir, *Man's Search for Meaning,* Frankl writes, "Don't aim for success—the more you aim at it and make it a target, the more you are going to miss it. For success, like happiness, cannot be pursued; it must ensue, and it only does so as the unintended side-effect of one's personal dedication to a cause greater than oneself. . . ." Frankl is proposing that the more we let go of externally defined work objectives, and the more we are liberated to experiment, to explore the byways of different working paths, the more likely we are to find the one that suits us best.

In a recently unearthed 1958 letter to a friend, twenty-one-year-old Hunter Thompson—among the last people you might think to turn to for safe career advice—challenged the friend to wake up, take charge, and find work that spoke to him. This applies to all of us, not just gonzo risk takers.

Each of us has a unique and deep-seated combination of beliefs, needs, desires, and sensibility—not necessarily wholly conscious, but nonetheless a vision—that guides our life. To do work out in the world, work that has consequence: entertaining people or changing their minds, helping them be healthier or more content, designing useful algorithms or clever new devices or beautiful clothing, getting rich or being the first earthling to walk on Mars. And if we're conscious of those dreams, if we work at it and keep them at the top of our minds, and we're lucky, they drive us to make certain choices—to go to art school, study engineering, become a lawyer . . . or intern at NASA or SpaceX.

Back in the eighteenth century, the Swiss mathematician Daniel Bernoulli approvingly suggested that people tend to make choices based less on quantifiable financial factors—this was a *mathematician*—and more on the projected emotional benefit of an outcome. The desire to be or to do good, to be engaged in work in which one feels real meaning and purpose, is key.

Deep down, people understand what matters most to them in a job. Nearly all of our thousands of survey respondents were very clear about what was most important to them in their work. And it wasn't just a title or status or paycheck. They ranked the drivers of happiness in their work as follows:

1. Feeling appreciated.
2. Work that brings out the best in me.
3. Experiencing/learning new things.
4. Meaningful work.

But we know that the everyday details and vicissitudes of life get in the way. Inertia, fear, paying the bills, or other pressures and setbacks cause us to give up our dreams. In the research for my last book, I came across a concept from psychology called "emotion labor." The labor part comes from the gap between how you feel at your most relaxed and natural and how you are obliged to act differently in different circumstances. When all cylinders are firing and we feel truly engaged and valued for the work we are doing, there is no gap between who we are and what we are doing. There is no emotion labor. When the gap between who we are and what we do for work is too great, trouble arises. For Thinkers and Defenders and Drifters—all of whom, according to the research for this book, are not so inclined to pay attention to their guts when making work decisions—reconnecting with what's personally meaningful can become a defining anchor around which they can take risks exploring new kinds of work.

> *The goal of the hero's journey is yourself, finding yourself.*
>
> **—JOSEPH CAMPBELL**

I think an upside to this moment of economic flux and volatility is that while old-fashioned set-and-forget career tracks are increasingly obsolete, if you can plausibly envision a particular kind of work that you want to be doing, chances are better than ever that you can figure out how to make it happen. So many of the forces that make our current world unsettling—digital transformation, outsourced project work, global competition, a premium on innovation and disruption—can work *for* you as well as against you.

The art of risk-taking is an odyssey of self-discovery. Finding and embracing your true north in your working life doesn't mean that you have to dedicate yourself to capital-I "Important" work like curing diabetes or launching the next Facebook. Meaning can be derived from running a cozy farm-to-table bed-and-breakfast, or making certain that your team's schedule always runs smoothly, or working in a job that guarantees you're always home for dinner and never miss a child's game or performance. The key is to develop confidence in what is most important to you and then to design your working life around that conviction.

It's important to remember that getting a clear fix on your occupational lodestar doesn't mean that your working life will thereafter be on a smooth, fixed track. Fixed career tracks are disappearing, autopiloting works for machines but not people, and everyone's life circumstances are fluid—in response to which we each must constantly respond, adapt, change. In his memoir, *The Night of the Gun,* David Carr chose to go public in a big, risky way with a kind of personal truth telling that was brave for a *New York Times* reporter. "As Whitman suggested," David told me, "we all 'contain multitudes,' and [my] history is a part of who I am." Proceeding through life with his worst secrets "already manifest—there is something to be said for that." Working from your core outward and being true to yourself simply means learning to align the values *you* consider important as best you can with what you're good at and what you get paid to do. And realigning them again and again and again throughout your life.

> *The essence of bravery is being without self-deception.*
>
> **—PEMA CHÖDRÖN**

RULES FOR STAYING TRUE TO YOURSELF

Be Clear About What You Want

Serial entrepreneur and brilliant thinker Seth Godin has been called "America's Greatest Marketer" by *American Way* magazine. I consider him the apotheosis of what it means to be a Pioneer. He's founded multiple companies, most of which he readily admits have failed. Yoyodyne, his first Internet company—named after a fictional company in Thomas Pynchon's dark novels—pioneered "permission marketing," allowing consumers to *request* marketing messages. It was one of Seth's companies that didn't fail; he sold it to Yahoo! in 1998, at the height of the first dot.com bubble. He's written eighteen books that have been translated into more than thirty languages—but most of his content is *given away for free* in order to build the huge, cultlike audience of devotees who attend his highly lucrative public lectures and presentations. In a recent book, *We Are All Weird,* he advocates that marketers offer consumers more options and encourage them to make buying choices based on their idiosyncratic tastes and values.

But for all his risky professional experiments, successful and not, when I asked him about his biggest professional risk, he didn't hesitate. "For me," he says, "it was choosing to fire my company's biggest client." At the time, in 1992, his book-packaging company, Seth Godin Productions, had only six employees, and their largest client accounted for more than half the revenues. It was a young company and, Seth says, "I felt we might fold at any moment."

Oddly, the problem stemmed from Seth being *too* success-ful working on behalf of the big client. He'd put together and sold a multititle book project for them that was lucrative and difficult to manage. "It was an organization," he says of the client, "that was already good at being difficult, one that brought a sharp pencil and little humanity to every interac-tion." After many months, it became clear to Seth that if he kept working with them, "we would become an organization that was good at dealing with difficult clients. If we could sur-vive this, the thinking went, then we could survive anyone." The thing is, he says, "I didn't want to build an organization that was good at dealing with difficult clients."

So Seth walked away, taking a huge financial hit. "It was crazy. The good news is that we were energized by our free-dom and the lack of finger-pointing and nastiness. And made back the lost business in less than two months."

Turn Avocation into Vocation

I don't know if Helene Godin was Seth-like before she mar-ried him or if decades of marriage to a do-what-you-*love* Pio-neer shaped her, but her professional trajectory illustrates how a lifelong Thinker discovered a passion by finding and unleashing her inner Pioneer. In 2010, Helene was working as in-house counsel at a major information services company. Her hours were long and the satisfaction low. "It wasn't my employer that was the problem," she says. "It was a shift in the profession. The *craft* of lawyering was gone. It was now all about generating documents as quickly as possible. So I quit. Without a plan."

She was forty-eight. "I suddenly found myself at the super-market several times a week," she says of her period of unem-ployment. "While working as a lawyer, it was more likely to be a once-a-month occurrence at best. I noticed that 'gluten free' had started to gain traction. The amount of shelf space the gluten-free products were getting was expanding with each market visit." That's when the lightbulb went off for her.

When she had thought about her "second act," as she calls it, operating a bakery had not been at the top of her list. In fact, it wasn't on the list at all. She'd toyed with the idea of becoming a literary agent—plausible, even obvious, given that agents use many of the same skills as lawyers—but then she'd realized the very plausibility of the shift made it unappealing, since "wasn't that just like being a lawyer?" She'd spent twenty years working in law firms and legal departments, and what she really, deeply wanted, she'd come to understand, was to open a small business in her "charming little town" on the Hudson River in suburban New York.

"I had never worked in a restaurant, and wasn't even the one responsible for making dinner every night—that was my husband's role. It was his way of unwinding at the end of the day. But I loved *thinking* about food. I loved planning menus. I loved setting the table and plating each course. I also loved hosting dinner parties." She is nothing if not vivacious. A res-taurant would have fit the bill, but "it was too daunting a proposition, with extremely long hours and the need to de-velop too wide an array of products. A bakery seemed like a much more manageable proposition." And based on her *aha!* moment at the supermarket, she hatched a plan: a gluten-free vegan bakery. But first she had to learn how to, you know . . . bake.

She created her own virtual cooking school. "I spent ten to twelve hours a day researching everything I could about conventional baking, gluten-free baking, and vegan baking—although I quickly discovered that eggs were an essential ingredient in *my* recipes." So she abandoned the vegan idea but still omitted the dairy. "Putting what I had learned to the test, I started baking like a demon. Bake. Bite. Throw out. Until I figured out what worked. It was similar to the problem solving I had done as a lawyer, but I enjoyed it even more."

She opened By the Way Bakery in May 2011. "Every day I offer my customers, each of whom I think of as my guest, an array of beautiful sweets, displayed in just the right way in my adorable little shop. And that makes me very happy." Business is booming—and she's just opened a second shop, in Manhattan.

Do What You Know to Be Right

At fifty, Sallie Krawcheck has run Smith Barney and the global wealth management divisions of both Citigroup and Bank of America. More than once during the last dozen years, she was called "the most powerful woman on Wall Street." She took what she describes as her biggest professional risk—in an industry explicitly all about assessing, taking, and avoiding risks—in her mid-thirties, when she was director of research for Sanford C. Bernstein & Co. "My firm," she says, "was a research firm, and I and my team took us out of the underwriting business"—that is, the raising of capital and issuing of stock for companies—"on the view that this business served as a conflict of interest, in which the most bullish [analysts] were typically the highest paid." The financial implications of Sallie's very risky decision were immediate. "We lost millions of dollars of revenues. Our competitors and our clients told us we were misguided, and we lost any number of employees, since they could be paid more by companies that remained in the underwriting business." But her conviction that she had done the right thing was vindicated when New York State "investigations revealed the conflicts [in other firms] and our business ultimately benefited." Sallie found meaning and career direction by sticking to her core values. And now she's left the financial industry, devoting herself full-time to a mission-driven for-profit business that produces events to train and network high-achieving women: In 2013, she bought 85 Broads, a pun on the New York financial district address of Goldman Sachs, and rebranded the company Ellevate.

Help Yourself by Helping Others

Elizabeth Scharpf, thirty-seven, is a former Notre Dame basketball player and Harvard Business School graduate. Her desire for meaning—a passion to improve the world—drove her to invent a new kind of business from scratch. At HBS, she thought she might use her MBA to pursue a career in biotech at a start-up or in Big Pharma or maybe doing consulting work in international development. But in 2005, while interning for the World Bank in Mozambique, Scharpf was shocked to overhear a colleague bemoaning the widespread problem of women who missed work during their monthly periods.

Stunned, she began to dig into the problem and found a heart-breaking but stunningly simple reason the women were missing days and losing income: They couldn't afford menstrual pads. Working women in twenty-first-century Mozambique, she discovered, were routinely reduced to using ineffective rags, or in rural areas even bark or mud, for feminine hygiene. And she discovered it was a problem throughout the poorest parts of the developing world. In countries where the per capita GDP is only a few dollars a day, the $3 a month it might cost to buy pads was a barrier to individual progress across the board—education, jobs, advancement. And because the very subject of menstruation seems "taboo" or "icky," it was a major lost opportunity for lifting poor women and thus their poor countries out of poverty. "I have empathy for these women," Scharpf told me, "because I don't think where you are born should be the biggest indicator of your potential for health, wealth, and happiness. I want to change that dynamic."

She was galvanized. She decided to launch in Rwanda, where she identified processed banana-plant waste as a viable absorbent and thus a cheap way to manufacture pads locally at much lower cost than imported synthetic pads. She enlisted textile and manufacturing experts from MIT and North Carolina State University to help figure out the technology. She launched Sustainable Health Enterprises (SHE) in 2009 with seed money from a social entrepreneurship venture capital firm, Echoing Green. The business is doing well. Scharpf told me that "we've gone from using a household blender making absorbent fluff to figuring out industrial-scale pad production that suits an environment with little electricity and water. Now we are reaching thousands of girls in Rwanda with more affordable pads *and* the health information to keep them healthy and confident in school. Now we look to expansion." Hundreds of inquiries from twenty-five countries have come into SHE, inviting Elizabeth's enterprise to replicate its Rwandan model elsewhere.

Elizabeth intuitively understood a powerful motivator that the great developmental psychologist Erik Erikson called "generativity"—essentially the human motivation to help others. For what do we want to be remembered? Asking yourself this question regularly over the course of your working life will serve as a prod to stay true to your course. If you've wandered away, it's an opportunity to make the appropriate shifts.

Embrace the Impermanence

I think one welcome but little discussed corollary benefit of the new normal—the average American job now lasts only four years—is the regular opportunity to reevaluate our relationship with work. Is the job we've done for a while making full use of our skills and interests and personality, as they exist *now*? Does it give a sense of fulfillment and accomplishment? Sometimes the answers are no, no, no, no, and no. Which means that having many jobs or even multiple careers over the course of our twenty-first-century lives becomes a *positive* as well as a challenging prospect. When we don't count on the work we're doing today to be what we'll do *for the rest of our lives,* the prospect of letting go and experimenting with another kind of work becomes less terrifying. Knowing that we may continue to reinvent ourselves professionally can be reassuring. We can win some and lose some while understanding that over the long haul we can still find ourselves doing work that suits us better.

> *The greatest thing in the world is to know how to belong to yourself.*
>
> **—MICHEL DE MONTAIGNE, RENAISSANCE ESSAYIST**

Finding the right next job or career is about tuning in to your inner voice and zeroing in on your purpose. This is not an easy thing to do. The target is constantly shifting; we are different people at different stages of our life and different people in different circumstances. As the cultural anthropologist Mary Catherine Bateson writes in *Composing a Life,* life commitments are "continually refocused and redefined. We must invest time and passion in specific goals and yet at the same time acknowledge that these are mutable." Life is about change. Learn to embrace the flow. As Steve Jobs, the guru of all wannabe Pioneers, put it, "The only way to be truly satisfied is to do what you believe is great work. And the only way to do great work is to love what you do. If you haven't found it yet, keep looking. Don't settle. As with all matters of the heart, you'll know when you find it." And that's just it. We find (and do) our best work with our minds *and* our hearts.

David Carr

David Carr was a cultural critic and journalist, among the best of his generation, who wrote a column for *The New York Times*. He died at age fifty-eight in early 2015.

What's the most significant risk you've taken professionally?

DAVID CARR: Back when my twins were getting ready for college, it was clear that we had not done the financial footwork to help them with the terrifying costs. I decided it might help to do a memoir based on a personal history of addiction that involved some remarkably unsavory behavior. The book, *The Night of the Gun,* attempted to advance the genre of junkie memoir by reporting out my memories by doing videotaped interviews and digging into medical and legal records. It was, in retrospect, a very satisfying journalistic and literary endeavor, something that I felt good about. But given that I work at *The New York Times,* its portrait of a narcissistic and occasionally brutal man who eventually sobered up and gained custody of his children presented some, um, optical issues.

Specifically, what would my bosses think of not only the

book I had done, but the *things* that I had done? I can remember when a draft was finished, I went to my boss at the time, Sam Sifton, and he said he would walk it down to the [top] editors, but gently suggested it might be better if I was the one who delivered the manuscript. He was right, but I felt like putting on oven mitts or grabbing a pair of tongs to hand it off. As it turned out, Bill Keller, [at that time] the editor of the *Times,* thought the book was just fine. Probably not exactly his cup, but as he said—and I am paraphrasing—"We don't hire nuns. The work you did is carefully reported and reflects the standards that we have here at the paper."

I was and am proud of the book, and if it means that every once in a while someone who doesn't like me or my work dismisses me as a crackhead, I'm okay with that.

BECOMING A DISCIPLE OF EXPERIENCE

In his white button-down oxford shirt, narrow black tie, and white sneakers, the slightly chubby middle-aged man swaying center stage at Madison Square Garden, chanting, *"If we do it again, I'm going to freak out, freak out,"* is the ultimate alter-ego fantasy figure for a lot of men at the younger end of middle age, the Tom Cruise of *Risky Business* twenty, twenty-five years later. And the crowd bobbing and swaying to the ecstatic, new wave–y rhythm shrieks and stomps in defiance of those lyrics, begging the band to keep doing it again and again.

Following a three-hour performance at Madison Square Garden in 2011, James Murphy, the forty-one-year-old singer-songwriter, founder/producer of the immensely popular indie band LCD Soundsystem, quit performing. His group's albums were consistently well reviewed, and he was still two or three decades younger than all sorts of working rock stars. For his fans and the music world, the move was improbable bordering on inconceivable. Why stop when the going still seemed so good? When the fans were so ardent? What did Murphy fear he'd risk by continuing to perform? I wasn't at that concert, but my guess is he was afraid of becoming stale, of losing his edge, of mediocrity, of getting bored with the same old, same old—exactly the same reasons that catapult those of us in less high-profile or glamorous positions to dare to embark on something new. Far better for Murphy to begin anew springing from the *top* of his game.

The art of optimal risk-taking demands that we become internally attuned to the merest whiff of change on the horizon—that we have anticipated and prepared for the moment when our work inevitably transforms. For a guitarist, it might be recognizing that the arthritis will irrevocably compromise the virtuosity of his performance; for the CEO, to admit that the omnipresent exhaustion of constant travel has sapped her will to give 110 percent to her job; for the paperback book publisher, to switch gears into electronic publishing. It is precisely at these moments of looming major change that it's often the hardest to take risks—when the going is still good and the downhill slope is on the horizon. But if you've adopted the philosophy of risk-taking that I advocate, you'll be poised to take action at the right moment. Almost everything in life operates in cycles; there is no permanent peak performance or winning streak. A regular risk practice is essential to develop the acumen to understand when to stay and when to move.

Fred Wilson, the supersuccessful, super-plugged-in zillionaire founder of the venture capital firm Union Square Ventures, a major investor in Twitter and Foursquare, attended that final LCD Soundsystem concert. He was six months away from turning fifty and felt he was on Murphy's frequency. "As we watched the band put on a fantastic show last night," he wrote on his blog the next day, "I was thinking about going out on top. So few manage to do it. Shaq is warming the bench in Boston. Brett Favre should have called it quits after he threw the pick in OT against the Saints. The Stones haven't written a great song in thirty years. The money and the burning desire to 'win another one' drives the great ones to stick around too long.

"And I wondered if the rules of the entertainment and sports world can be applied to venture capital and startups. Is there a time to call it quits in business? I look at Warren Buffett . . . and I see individuals still enjoying the work and delivering for their shareholders and investors into their 80s.

"But I also look around the venture capital business and I see investors who were at the top of their games in the 90s struggling to remain relevant. And I think about how I want to manage this issue myself.

"How do you know when you've done your last great startup? How do you know when you've done your last great investment? How do you know when you don't have the drive, hunger, and insights to keep delivering top performance?

"Right now, coming off two weeks of totally relaxing vacation with my family, I find myself up early, thinking, writing, and planning. I don't sense it is yet time to hang up my cleats or walk off the stage like James Murphy did last night. But the thought is in my mind and I want it to stay there. The investment business is not easy. You are only as good as your last trade, fund, or year. And the venture capital business is particularly tricky. All the returns in the business accrue to the top ten or, at best, twenty percent of investors. When you lose your edge, your performance suffers, often badly. But it can take a decade for the rest of the world to notice because there is so much latency in the venture capital business.

"I don't want to be the investor who sticks around milking the investors for fee income and raising funds based on returns that are over a decade old. That's a Rolling Stones move and it is not for me. I'd prefer to do what James Murphy and his band did last night."

Three years later, Fred still hasn't pulled the rip cord out of his firm but tells me that for him the sentiment "is truer today than ever. Although I'm not about to retire, I certainly think about it from time to time." Like most of us in today's over-scheduled world, Fred feels "a tension between wanting to slow down and being scared of slowing down."

Tell me, what is it you plan to do with your one wild and precious life?

—MARY OLIVER, POET

Murphy, no stranger to risk-taking, had been committed to making music since his early twenties—actually turning down a once-in-a-lifetime chance for potential fame and fortune at *twenty-two* when he had a chance to become the first staff writer on *Seinfeld* in order to focus on his music. Rock and roll was his passion. And a lot of his lyrics asked the listener to focus on thorny life dilemmas, such as committing one's life to an unsustainable path without even realizing it. As Nitsuh Abebe put it in a review of LCD Soundsystem's final performance, "LCD's first single, 'Losing My Edge,' was a monologue in which the most clued-in person on the scene—the one with immaculate knowledge of the whole canon of vital underground music—watches his position get usurped by younger kids. It's a blithe parody, a hilarious in-joke that critics lapped up. But it's also an incredibly serious song about dedicating yourself to something ephemeral." It seems Murphy decided the optimal life span for a band was about a decade. He had talked the talk, and now—*it's been good!*—he was actually walking the walk. The lesson from Murphy is that it doesn't matter where you are in the arc of your career, whether you believe you've "arrived" or not, pushing yourself to take risks will ensure that your work continues to evolve and to feel purposeful.

Disbanding LCD Soundsystem didn't mean that Murphy quit working. He's continued to push his boundaries in a variety of new ways—producing Arcade Fire, recording songs with Outkast's Andre 3000, scoring music for Noah Baumbach's film *Greenberg,* directing his own short film, *Little Duck,* and blending a James Murphy signature coffee for the Brooklyn coffee shop Blue Bottle. And why? "I like learning," he told *Q* magazine. "I like to be a novice."

The point here is that deciding to leave a job or change a career isn't necessarily fueled by crisis or dissatisfaction. Stars such as James Murphy got successful in the first place by means of prescience and spectacularly good timing (as well as talent and hard work and luck), seeing ahead and around cultural and economic corners. And so at the tops of their games, they risk big changes in their working lives before the world forces their hands.

MOST ADAPTABLE = FITTEST

In a 2012 *Fast Company* cover story, the magazine's editor Robert Safian correctly described the essential contemporary mind-set as one that "embraces instability, that tolerates—and even enjoys—recalibrating careers, business models, and assumptions." He called those who embody it "Generation Flux." While I obviously agree with him about the differences between twenty-first-century and twentieth-century career modi operandi, I think his historical frame was too narrow. I think that the twentieth century was the aberrant blip, that the embrace of flux actually has a very old pedigree—a good five hundred or six hundred years old, in fact. The Renaissance had no magazine cover stories heralding and naming it at the time, but it was all about exceptional individuals moving beyond the stagnation and received wisdom of the Middle Ages, causing and welcoming instability, recalibrating assumptions as they'd never been recalibrated before, finding wholly new ways of thinking, inventing, building, doing business, working. Modern life started with the Renaissance, and the Renaissance came about by people recovering ancient wisdom and embracing and provoking flux.

The essential fuel that drove the vast cultural, scientific, and commercial innovation of the Renaissance and the subsequent Enlightenment was the multidisciplinary tendency of ambitious amateurs and tinkerers who didn't limit themselves to one narrow job description—such as Leonardo da Vinci (painter, sculptor, engineer, architect, inventor), Galileo Galilei (mathematician, philosopher, astronomer), Sir Walter Raleigh (explorer, poet, soldier), Thomas Jefferson (lawyer, farmer, revolutionary, inventor, architect). But this generalist polymath approach, where ambitious people were free to follow their curiosity and try to solve problems in any realm, went out of fashion during the last century or so. Partly it was the reemergence of powerful trade guilds—not unlike the ones, ironically, that had arisen in the Middle Ages. Our twentieth-century mania for credentialing and licensing professional and trade associations and unions would look familiar to the stonecutters and glassmakers and armorers of medieval Europe. Industrialization also made the old amateur spirit seem outmoded, since the quest for large-scale efficiency led inevitably to hyperspecialization. But we achieved productivity and prosperity at the great cost of suppressing people's natural tendencies to experiment and do more than one kind of work well. Today's Renaissance man (or woman) has become the remarked-upon exception.

> *What if we had a chance to do it again and again,*
> *until we finally did get it right? Wouldn't that be*
> *wonderful?*
>
> **—KATE ATKINSON, AUTHOR OF *LIFE AFTER LIFE***

Most of us stumble into our first jobs, and our careers take shape as a result of happenstance. And except for the rare few, such as the artistic or scientific masterminds among us, our occupational destiny is probably not some hidden treasure just waiting for the right key to unlock it. Rather, the working life each of us makes is assembled ad hoc along the way out of many possibilities determined by our needs, life stage, skills, interests, and opportunities, as well as by rapidly evolving economic, technological, and social realities—and by chance. Now that the average job lasts only a few years, how to think about the work we do has become a question we face anew again and again over the course of our lives, a matter of perpetually navigating and course correcting rather than making a single definitive choice at twenty and being towed along for the ride.

We need to make interdisciplinary learning fashionable again, because a variety of perspectives can inspire solutions adapted to different fields and new circumstances—to the not entirely foreseeable *next* job. Four hundred years ago, before America was America or the United States, it was the New World and it required people to invent entirely new lives. Then, two hundred years ago, the Industrial Revolution came along, and it was rough for people who'd worked the way they and their ancestors had for generations—but those who adapted thrived in the *new* New World. A hundred years ago, a third of Americans lived on farms and knew only farming, and as that number began shrinking precipitously (to just 2 percent today), it was wrenching for millions of people—but also enabled profound opportunities for my rural Kansas father and rural Nebraska father-in-law, who found new ways to earn better livings. But in 1815 and 1915, adaptation was a matter of learning one new specialty and sticking with it forever, of responding to the sudden game-changing insecurity by focusing on conventional *security*. Today, the game change and resulting challenges are just as profound, but crucially different: The career mind-set *this* century requires is about having multiple skills and learning to live a life of perpetual flexibility and course correction. What's required of working people in our twenty-first-century present is an MO more like the plucky, gritty, ultraindividualistic improvisation required of Americans in the eighteenth and early nineteenth centuries than how we've thought about work for the last century or so.

RISK/REWARD—TURNING INACTION INTO ACTION

Peter Thiel, one of the cofounders of PayPal, has a theory about adaptation. In a piece in *The Wall Street Journal,* he argued that our economy is still operating through the prism of nineteenth-century physicists, who believed "that all energy is evenly distributed and everything comes to rest—also known as the heat death of the universe. Whatever your views of thermodynamics, it is a powerful metaphor. In business, equilibrium means stasis, and stasis means death." And not just in business, in every individual working life. To avoid stasis, risks must be taken. Moreover, according to Sonja Lyubomirsky, a psychologist at the University of California, Riverside, the act of committing to goals also provides a structure and meaning to our lives that leads to more overall happiness. She quotes G. K. Chesterton in this regard: "There is one thing which gives radiance to everything. It is the idea of something around the corner." And as I've said again and again in this book, the new world of work is seldom a matter of committing to just one narrowly defined goal, but rather a series of goals, a lifelong decathlon of your own design.

The people in our final Risk/Reward survey understand this. When asked an open-ended question about what their dream work would be, almost all of the 650 respondents had no trouble answering the question. People working in places as disparate as warehouses, banks, hospitals, real estate agencies, public relations firms, and financial organizations had very clearly defined ideas about the kinds of jobs they would find most fulfilling. The responses include a surprising number of people who want to open no-kill animal shelters or become veterinarians. Others want to become psychiatrists, marine biologists, teachers, park rangers, and—no doubt inspired by the infinitely replicating *CSI* shows—forensic scientists. Some people were incredibly specific about the dream jobs they envision—"a Cajun chef at a high-end New Orleans restaurant," a "first surgical assistant," an artist at Pixar, someone eager to "drive the bus at Disney World." I am heartened by the enthusiasm in people's responses. Most of the jobs were attainable——and many don't require advanced professional degrees. A police officer in our survey who's interested in becoming a professional genealogist can start with her own family's chart and expand from there. The customer service rep who wants to become a social worker can volunteer for a local hotline.

The requirement for many people to move toward their dream jobs is actually pretty simple. The most important step is to internalize and reinforce the belief that a regular practice of measured risk-taking is the means to the end. Johann Wolfgang von Goethe made a strong case two hundred years ago for risk-taking in *Faust:*

> Then indecision brings its own delays,
> And days are lost lamenting o'er lost days.
> Are you in earnest? Seize this very minute;
> What you can do, or dream you can, begin it;
> Boldness has genius, power and magic in it.

The majority of people in our surveys and my interviews who have made some kind of scary-seeming work-related move—from quitting a job before having another to working remotely—know this power and believe it has worked out well. To move past our fears, to build the working lives we want, we must learn to take action. Moving forward requires us to maintain a continual conversation between our inner Spock and inner Kirk, between the data and our emotions.

> *We must be willing to get rid of the life we've planned, so as to have the life that is waiting for us.*
>
> **—JOSEPH CAMPBELL**

RISK AND RESILIENCE

And speaking of cinematic space opera, in Alfonso Cuarón's super-realistic 2013 film, *Gravity,* Sandra Bullock plays an accomplished midcareer medical engineer but novice astronaut, sent into space as a so-called mission specialist. George Clooney is the veteran astronaut accompanying her. Early in the film, Bullock and Clooney are outside their space shuttle in zero gravity, tethered to the Hubble telescope, installing new equipment—when a shower of satellite debris crashes into them, severing Bullock's tether and blowing her off into space. Severed from her umbilical link, she spins end over terrifying end, farther and farther away from Clooney, safety, anything remotely familiar, life. Unbound by gravity, she has no ability to alter her trajectory and, with no point of reference in the infinity of space, not even a clue where to focus her attention. Her panic is our panic.

The commonplace take of critics and other writers has been that *Gravity* is a film about asking us to confront our mortality. And while that's true, I think there's a different, more timely and actionable message. The movie's metaphoric power derives not only from the obvious and ultimate binary condition of death versus struggling to live. To me it is also rich with metaphors for life in the workplace and political economy of the early twenty-first century. Bullock and Clooney are *working* when disaster strikes, doing their unremarkable technical jobs in an extraordinary place. Bullock is every(wo)man, after a mere six months of training thrust into circumstances beyond her competency—like many of us struggling to keep up with technological innovations beyond our skill or real understanding. The incoming satellite debris that wrecks their spacecraft enacts in heightened reality something we all intuitively know, that the most sophisticated technologies and systems and the most thoroughly developed contingency plans can be rendered moot by something as simple as a storm surge, a loosened bolt, a new means of selling. A career years in the making and years on the right track can be sideswiped and blown up practically in an instant by events beyond anyone's control—a company downsizing or being acquired or going out of business, the introduction of a disruptive new technology, impossible competition from overseas, a cancer diagnosis. I could go on.

> A *warrior begins to take responsibility for the direction of her life.*
>
> **—PEMA CHÖDRÖN**

Bullock, alone in the vastness of space, is adrift without guidance (management) or infrastructure (familiar contacts) or skills, left to scramble alone, totally alone, breathlessly improvising solutions as each new crisis unfolds, with her oxygen (salary) running out. The message is clear for all of us battling the odds, figuring out what to do next given the strange, futuristic, and often terrifying new conditions in which we find ourselves. Yes, we are ultimately alone in making our working lives *work,* but if we turn inward, get in touch with our instincts, *and* consult the manuals, remain resilient and composed, we can triumph.

So it is with our working lives. We apprentice, we date, we quit jobs, we marry, our kids leave home, we launch companies, we divorce, we take time off, we start new careers, a hobby becomes a paying job, and so on and on—we stretch and contract according to opportunity and dreams and the vicissitudes that life hurls our way.

We live in times that are not easy for the complacent or faint of heart. Charting a working life today requires courage and determination and course correction amid the onslaught of new circumstances beyond our control and highly imperfect intelligence about even the near future. Each of us must learn to build our own life rafts, devise ad hoc means of survival, have contingency plans and also the readiness to revise or throw out those contingency plans on the fly.

But while one's work and career is a high-stakes enterprise, and a part of life in which planning and systematically developing the right habits of mind are most possible and essential, it is usually not a matter of life and death. And unlike an astronaut lost in space, we are really not alone. There are millions of us charting new, independent ways of earning a living by doing work we care about, establishing alliances and co-working spaces, providing free access to resources, building new networks, new products, and new strategies for blending work and life in this radically new age. Psychologically, this unfamiliar gray zone between what was and what is to be can be a difficult or even disturbing one to inhabit.

The key to personal progress is adopting the mind-set that we are each a scientist pursuing by trial and error the grand experiment that is our life. Learning to test hypotheses, to try things beyond the familiar or obvious, to probe our not-quite-conscious desires and aversions, to meet new people and enter new contexts, to risk failure—these habits can lead us to connect with the kind of work that will make us most content. We each need to become what Leonardo da Vinci called "a disciple of experience."

ACKNOWLEDGMENTS

......................................▶

Writing this book has been a wonderful expedition of discovery. In fact, the process of research and writing it has been one apt model for how to risk in small and large ways: Approach people you don't know and ask for their time, create new research tools, be willing to rework the book again and again until it's what it should be.

Mark Truss's and Heather Field's significant risk—devoting their time, brainpower, and deep know-how to this pro bono project—provided a huge reward to me (if not them): the data at the heart of the book.

The generosity of spirit of the dozens of people I interviewed over the course of three years of research—and their willingness to expose their intimate hopes, dreams, and failures—was essential to giving shape and substance to the book. *Thank you,* Mike Ananny, Kristi Andersen, David Boghossian, Po Bronson, Carolyn Brooks, Peter Brown, Tory Burch, David Carr, Rosanne Cash, Stephen Chao, Jim Cramer, Kerrin Degnan, Whitney Donaldson, Benjamin Dyett,

Sasha Emerson, John Eyler, Ingrid Fetell, Jon Fine, Helene Godin, Seth Godin, Danny Goldberg, Ben Goldberger, Philippa Gordon, Maura Grogan, Margaret Hamburg, Carla Hendra, Daisy Jenkins, Derek John, Nadia Jones, Maira Kalman, Barbara Kass, Lydia Kauer, Elizabeth Kennedy, Leslie Koch, Danica Kombol, Sallie Krawcheck, David Lewis, Ashley Merryman, Christopher Meyer, Zanele Mutepfa, Jane Pauley, Matt Pearson, Thomas Petruso, Anna Quindlen, Andrea Miller Raisfeld, George Raisfeld, Deondrae Rhone, Margaret Roach, Melissa Rothberg, Stephan Sagmeister, Sheryl Sandberg, Elizabeth Scharpf, Gail Scovell, Nell Scovell, Ted Scovell, Mindy Shapiro, Bonnie Siegler, Debbie Slater, Brian Smith, Elizabeth Spiers, Stephan Stohler, Sabira Taher, Daniel Thorson, Emily Thorson, Kjerstin Thorson, Laurel Touby, Jane Von Mehren, Ken Von Mehren, Lucas Von Mehren, Susan Walthop-Pope, Fred Wilson, and Joanne Wilson.

My agent, Suzanne Gluck, has been the ideal enabler from the beginning. Jane Von Mehren took the first leap of faith with the subject, and Julie Grau and Jessica Sindler guided me through the homestretch with grace and enthusiasm. The team at Random House has been exceptional: Gina Centrello, Tom Perry, Sally Marvin, London King, Leigh Marchant, Laura Van der Veer, and Joseph Perez. Danica Kombol, Emily Berry, and Akiko Busch were excellent guinea-pig readers of various drafts; their suggestions always moved the ball forward. And as ever, my family has been integral: Kate for allowing me to chronicle her risk-taking in real time, Lucy for making me laugh and keeping it real, and Kurt for his unwavering devotion to helping me craft the best book imaginable.

I owe an enormous debt to the Civitella Ranieri Foundation, which provided me uninterrupted time to finish the book on the grounds of a castle in Umbria in the company of artists from around the world. Thank you, Dana Prescott and my fellow travelers, for making that final stretch the best ever.

BIBLIOGRAPHY

Amabile, Teresa, and Steven Kramer. *The Progress Principle: Using Small Wins to Ignite Joy, Engagement, and Creativity at Work*. Boston: Harvard Business Review Press, 2011.

Anker, Patty Chang. *Some Nerve: Lessons Learned While Becoming Brave*. New York: Riverhead Books, 2013.

Ariely, Dan. *The Upside of Irrationality: The Unexpected Benefits of Defying Logic at Work and at Home*. New York: HarperCollins, 2010.

Arment, Ben. *Dream Year: Make the Leap from a Job You Hate to a Life You Love*. New York: Portfolio/Penguin, 2014.

Bacal, Jessica. *Mistakes I Made at Work: 25 Influential Women Reflect on What They Got Out of Getting It Wrong*. New York: Plume, 2014.

Bateson, Mary Catherine. *Composing a Life*. New York: Penguin Books, 1990.

Bono, Edward De. *Six Thinking Hats*. Boston: Little, Brown, 1985.

Brabandere, Luc de, and Alan Iny. *Thinking in New Boxes: A New Paradigm for Business Creativity*. New York: Random House, 2013. Audiobook.

Bridges, William. *Managing Transitions: Making the Most of Change.* Reading, MA: Addison-Wesley, 1991.

Brockman, John. *This Explains Everything: Deep, Beautiful, and Elegant Theories of How the World Works.* New York: Harper Perennial, 2013.

———. *This Will Make You Smarter: New Scientific Concepts to Improve Your Thinking.* New York: Harper Perennial, 2012.

Bronson, Po. *What Should I Do with My Life?* New York: Random House, 2002.

———, and Ashley Merryman. *Top Dog: The Science of Winning and Losing.* New York: Twelve, 2013.

Campbell, Joseph, and Diane K. Osbon. *A Joseph Campbell Companion: Reflections on the Art of Living.* New York: Harper Perennial, 1998.

Carr, David. *The Night of the Gun: A Reporter Investigates the Darkest Story of His Life, His Own.* New York: Simon & Schuster, 2008.

Christensen, Clayton M., James Allworth, and Karen Dillon. *How Will You Measure Your Life?* New York: Harper Business, 2012.

Coates, John. *The Hour Between Dog and Wolf: Risk-Taking, Gut Feelings, and the Biology of Boom and Bust.* New York: Penguin Press, 2012.

Conley, Dalton. *Elsewhere, U.S.A.* New York: Pantheon Books, 2009.

Crampton, Norman J. *Boomer Men Working: Strategies for Staying Employed (or Tackling Unemployment).* Deadwood, OR: Wyatt-MacKenzie Publishing, 2012.

Damasio, Antonio R. *Descartes' Error: Emotion, Reason, and the Human Brain.* New York: Putnam, 1994.

Deutschman, Alan. *Change or Die: The Three Keys to Change at Work and in Life.* New York: Regan, 2007.

Dweck, Carol S. *Mindset: The New Psychology of Success*. New York: Random House, 2006.

Erikson, Erik H. *The Life Cycle Completed*. London: W. W. Norton & Co., 1998.

Fels, Anna. *Necessary Dreams: Ambition in Women's Changing Lives*. New York: Pantheon Books, 2004.

Frankl, Viktor E. *Man's Search for Meaning*. Boston: Beacon Press, 2006.

Galinsky, Lara, Kelly Nuxoll, Lance Armstrong, Doug Ulman, Geoffrey Canada, and Tony Deifell. *Work on Purpose*. New York: Echoing Green, 2011.

Gallagher, Winifred. *Rapt: Attention and the Focused Life*. New York: Penguin Press, 2009.

Gawande, Atul. *The Checklist Manifesto: How to Get Things Right*. New York: Metropolitan Books, 2010.

Gerson, Kathleen. *The Unfinished Revolution: How a New Generation Is Reshaping Family, Work, and Gender in America*. New York: Oxford University Press, 2010.

Gibson, D. W. *Not Working: People Talk About Losing a Job and Finding Their Way in Today's Changing Economy*. New York: Penguin Books, 2012.

Gigerenzer, Gerd. *Calculated Risks: How to Know When Numbers Deceive You*. New York: Simon & Schuster, 2002.

———. *Risk Savvy: How to Make Good Decisions*. New York: Viking, 2014.

Gilbert, Daniel Todd. *Stumbling on Happiness*. New York: Alfred A. Knopf, 2006.

Gill, Libby. *You Unstuck: Mastering the New Rules of Risk-Taking in Work and Life*. Palo Alto, CA: Solas House, 2009.

Gino, Francesca. *Sidetracked: Why Our Decisions Get Derailed, and How We Can Stick to the Plan*. Boston: Harvard Business Review Press, 2013.

Glei, Jocelyn K., and Scott Belsky. *Maximize Your Potential: Grow Your Expertise, Take Bold Risks and Build an Incredible Career*. Las Vegas: Amazon Publishing, 2013.

Goleman, Daniel. *Focus: The Hidden Driver of Excellence*. New York: HarperCollins, 2013.

Grossman, Richard L. *Choosing & Changing: A Guide to Self-Reliance*. New York: Dutton, 1978.

Hacker, Jacob S. *The Great Risk Shift: The Assault on American Jobs, Families, Health Care, and Retirement and How You Can Fight Back*. Oxford: Oxford University Press, 2006.

Heath, Chip, and Dan Heath. *Switch: How to Change Things When Change Is Hard*. New York: Broadway Books, 2010.

Hecht, Jennifer Michael. *The Happiness Myth: Why What We Think Is Right Is Wrong: A History of What Really Makes Us Happy*. San Francisco: HarperSanFrancisco, 2007.

Hertz, Noreena. *Eyes Wide Open: How to Make Smart Decisions in a Confusing World*. New York: Harper Business, 2013.

Hoffman, Reid, and Ben Casnocha. *The Start-Up of You*. New York: Crown Business, 2012.

Horowitz, Sara, and Toni Sciarra Poynter. *The Freelancer's Bible: Everything You Need to Know to Have the Career of Your Dreams on Your Terms*. New York: Workman Publishing, 2012.

Huffington, Arianna. *On Becoming Fearless: In Love, Work, and Life*. New York: Little, Brown, 2006.

Ibarra, Herminia. *Working Identity: Unconventional Strategies for Reinventing Your Career*. Boston: Harvard Business School Press, 2003.

Kahneman, Daniel. *Thinking, Fast and Slow*. New York: Farrar, Straus and Giroux, 2011.

Kay, Katty, and Claire Shipman. *The Confidence Code: The Science*

and Art of Self-Assurance—What Women Should Know.
New York: Harper Business, 2014.

Kolbell, Erik. *When Your Life Is On Fire: Thirteen Extraordinary People Answer One Simple Question.* Louisville, KY: Westminster John Knox, 2014.

Konnikova, Maria. *Mastermind: How to Think Like Sherlock Holmes.* New York: Viking, 2013.

Krogerus, Mikael, Roman Tschäppeler, and Jenny Piening. *The Decision Book: Fifty Models for Strategic Thinking.* New York: W. W. Norton & Co., 2012.

Krznaric, Roman. *How to Find Fulfilling Work.* New York: Picador, 2013.

Levine, Suzanne Braun. *Inventing the Rest of Our Lives: Women in Second Adulthood.* New York: Viking, 2005.

Lewis, Sarah Elizabeth. *The Rise: Creativity, the Gift of Failure, and the Search for Mastery.* New York: Simon & Schuster, 2014.

Lyubomirsky, Sonja. *The How of Happiness: A Scientific Approach to Getting the Life You Want.* New York: Penguin Press, 2008.

Malouf, David. *The Happy Life: The Search for Contentment in the Modern World.* New York: Pantheon Books, 2011.

Mandell, Lisa Johnson. *Career Comeback: Repackage Yourself to Get the Job You Want.* New York: Springboard Press, 2010.

Maurer, Robert. *One Small Step Can Change Your Life: The Kaizen Way.* New York: Workman Publishing, 2004.

McArdle, Megan. *The Up Side of Down: Why Failing Well Is the Key to Success.* New York: Viking, 2014.

McKeown, Greg. *Essentialism.* New York: Crown Business, 2014.

Miller, Caroline Adams, and Michael B. Frisch. *Creating Your Best Life: The Ultimate Life List Guide.* New York: Sterling, 2009.

Moretti, Enrico. *The New Geography of Jobs*. Boston: Houghton Mifflin Harcourt, 2012.

Palmer, Kimberly. *The Economy of You: Discover Your Inner Entrepreneur and Recession-Proof Your Life*. New York: AMACOM, 2014.

Patterson, Kerry. *Influencer: The New Science of Leading Change*, 2nd ed. New York: McGraw-Hill Companies, 2013.

Pauley, Jane. *Your Life Calling: Reimagining Your Life Now*. New York: Simon & Schuster, 2014.

Peck, Don. *Pinched: How the Great Recession Has Narrowed Our Futures and What We Can Do About It*. New York: Crown Publishing Group, 2011.

Peters, Thomas J. *The Little Big Things: 163 Ways to Pursue Excellence*. New York: HarperStudio, 2010.

Pink, Daniel H. *Drive: The Surprising Truth About What Motivates Us*. New York: Riverhead Books, 2009.

———. *A Whole New Mind: Why Right-Brainers Will Rule the Future*. New York: Riverhead Books, 2005.

Quindlen, Anna. *One True Thing*. New York: Random House, 1994.

Ricard, Matthieu. *Happiness: A Guide to Developing Life's Most Important Skill*. New York: Little, Brown, 2006.

Riesman, David, Reuel Denney, and Nathan Glazer. *The Lonely Crowd: A Study of the Changing American Character*. New Haven: Yale University Press, 1955.

Robin, Vicki, Joseph R. Dominguez, and Monique Tilford. *Your Money or Your Life: 9 Steps to Transforming Your Relationship with Money and Achieving Financial Independence*. New York: Penguin Books, 2008.

Saval, Nikil. *Cubed: A Secret History of the Workplace*. New York: Doubleday, 2014.

Schenck, Dwain. *Reset: How to Beat the Job Loss Blues and Get Ready for Your Next Act*. Boston: Da Capo Press, 2014.

Schumacher, E. F. *Good Work*. New York: Harper & Row, 1979.

———. *Small Is Beautiful: Economics as if People Mattered*. New York: Harper & Row, 1973.

Schwartz, Barry. *The Paradox of Choice: Why More Is Less*. New York: Ecco, 2004.

Schwartz, Tony, Jean Gomes, and Catherine McCarthy. *Be Excellent at Anything: The Four Keys to Transforming the Way We Work and Live*. New York: Free Press, 2011.

Seligman, Martin E. P. *Flourish: A Visionary New Understanding of Happiness and Well-Being*. New York: Free Press, 2011.

Sheehy, Gail. *New Passages: Mapping Your Life Across Time*. New York: Random House, 1995.

Sher, Barbara, and Barbara Smith. *I Could Do Anything if I Only Knew What It Was: How to Discover What You Really Want and How to Get It*. New York: Delacorte Press, 1994.

Shipman, Claire, and Katty Kay. *Womenomics: Write Your Own Rules for Success: How to Stop Juggling and Struggling and Finally Start Living and Working the Way You Really Want*. New York: Harper Business, 2009.

Siegel, Daniel J. *Mindsight: The New Science of Personal Transformation*. New York: Bantam Books, 2010.

Smith, Brian, Jackie Cuscuna, Lauren Kaelin, and Lucy Schaeffer. *Ample Hills Creamery: Secrets and Stories from Brooklyn's Favorite Ice Cream Shop*. New York: Stewart, Tabori & Chang, 2014.

Streep, Peg, and Alan B. Bernstein. *Mastering the Art of Quitting: Why It Matters in Life, Love, and Work*. Boston: Da Capo Press, 2014.

Sundheim, Doug. *Taking Smart Risks: How Sharp Leaders Win When Stakes Are High*. New York: McGraw-Hill, 2013.

Terkel, Studs. *Working: People Talk About What They Do All Day and How They Feel About What They Do*. New York: Pantheon Books, 1974.

Thaler, Richard H., and Cass R. Sunstein. *Nudge: Improving Decisions About Health, Wealth, and Happiness.* New Haven: Yale University Press, 2008.

Tillich, Paul. *The Courage to Be*. New Haven: Yale University Press, 1952.

Tracy, Brian. *Maximum Achievement: The Proven System of Strategies and Skills That Will Unlock Your Hidden Powers to Succeed*. New York: Simon & Schuster, 1993.

Webb, Maynard, and Carlye Adler. *Rebooting Work: Transform How You Work in the Age of Entrepreneurship*. San Francisco: Jossey-Bass, 2013.

Weisbrode, Kenneth. *On Ambivalence: The Problems and Pleasures of Having It Both Ways*. Cambridge, MA: MIT Press, 2012.

Williams, John. *Screw Work, Let's Play: How to Do What You Love and Get Paid for It*. Harlow, UK: Prentice Hall Business, 2010.

Yost, Cali Williams. *Work + Life: Finding the Fit That's Right for You*. New York: Riverhead Books, 2004.

Zweig, David. *Invisibles: The Power of Anonymous Work in an Age of Relentless Self-Promotion*. New York: Portfolio/Penguin, 2014.

ABOUT THE AUTHOR

ANNE KREAMER is the author of *It's Always Personal: Navigating Emotion in the New Workplace* and *Going Gray: What I Learned about Beauty, Sex, Work, Motherhood, Authenticity, and Everything Else That Really Matters.* She has been a columnist for *Fast Company* and *Martha Stewart Living,* and is a regular contributor to *Harvard Business Review.* Her work has appeared in *Time, The New York Times, The Wall Street Journal, Real Simple,* and *Travel & Leisure.* Previously, she was executive vice president and worldwide creative director for the television channels Nickelodeon and Nick at Nite. She graduated from Harvard College and lives in Brooklyn with her husband.

To inquire about booking Anne Kreamer for a speaking engagement, please contact the Penguin Random House Speakers Bureau at speakers@penguinrandomhouse.com.

www.annekreamer.com
Facebook.com/annekreamer
@annekreamer

ABOUT THE TYPE

This book was set in Sabon, a typeface designed by the well-known German typographer Jan Tschichold (1902–74). Sabon's design is based upon the original letter forms of sixteenth-century French type designer Claude Garamond and was created specifically to be used for three sources: foundry type for hand composition, Linotype, and Monotype. Tschichold named his typeface for the famous Frankfurt typefounder Jacques Sabon (c. 1520–80).